OUR LIVES AND HOPES

Our Lives and Hopes
Beyond Statistics and Reports

**Mridu Shailaj Thanki
and Jyoti Dhingra**

with children from slums in Dhaka

 The University Press Limited

The University Press Limited
Red Crescent House
61 Motijheel C/A
G. P. O. Box 2611
Dhaka 1000
Bangladesh
Fax: 8802 956 5443
E-mail: upl@bttb.net.bd, upl@bangla.net
Website: www.uplbooks.com

First published 2006

Cover & Illustrations: Children from slums in Dhaka

Cover produced by Ashraful Hassan Arif

ISBN 984 05 1759 7

Published by Mohiuddin Ahmed, The University Press Limited, Dhaka 1000. Computer design by Md. Nazmul Haque and produced by Abarton, 99 Malibagh, Dhaka. Printed at the Akota Offset Press, 119 Fakirapool, Dhaka, Bangladesh.

For Parents and Children,
Ours and
All Others'

Contents

Where do people earn per capita income?
More than one poor starving soul would like to know.
In our countries, numbers live better than people.
How many people prosper in times of prosperity?
How many people find their lives developed by
development?

— *Eduardo Galeano*

Glossary

Apa	Elder sister
Baksheesh	Tip, alms
Basti	slum
Bhalo hobe	Will be good
Bhalo	Good
Bodolog	Rich or powerful people
Crore	10 million
Darban	Guard
Desh	village to which one belongs
Eid	Muslim festival
Ekushey	The 21st of February, National Language Day
Gondogola	Rowdiness
Hartal	Strike during which the entire city life comes to a standstill
Kagoj	Paper, cardboard
Kala manush	Evil person
Khala	Aunt, mother's sister
Kharaab	Bad
Kuccha	Flimsy, weak
Kuppi	Small kerosene lamp
Mama	Mother's brother
Manush	Person
Mastaan	Local mafia member

Namaz	Prayers offered by Muslims
Nana	Maternal grandfather
Nani	Maternal grandmother
Pakka	Solid; made of bricks and cement
Pilao	Fried rice with meat or vegetables
Qurbani Eid	Eid during which sacrifices take place
Rangbaj	Men engaged in anti-social activities
Roza Eid	Eid that comes after one month of fasting
Shemai	Sweet made with vermicelli, sugar and milk
Shutki Bhartha	Dish made of small dried fish

Names of those who shared their lives with us have been changed to protect their privacy.

The statistics used in the book are from the years 2003 or before, the figures might have changed in the following years.

Acknowledgements

This book has been a journey made possible with the help of many people. Although it is impossible to convey our thanks to all of these people in mere words, we would like to express our appreciation for their contributions.

First and foremost we are much in debt to the children who without reserve shared their life experiences and insights into the world around them, giving this book its substance. Also we are extremely grateful to the parents and the families of the children who participated in this book for their trust, warmth and hospitality towards us, and their confidence in this effort.

Our heartfelt thanks to Mr. Chitto Halder for facilitating the whole process at the school and providing the support when needed; also thanks to Mr. Mahabub and Mr. Imam who provided help with the translations. To the board of the school we express our gratitude for permitting us to carry out this research work.

To Mr. AKM Mustak Ali and other staff of Integrated Community and Industrial Development in Bangladesh, who helped us understand the conditions of street children in Dhaka, we are thankful for their time and the insights provided by them.

Words of encouragement from friends and colleagues kept us going, despite the setbacks and the hardships. To all these friends we wish many thanks for their confidence in us.

Although they get mentioned last, our families have been with us in this from the beginning. We are obliged to Priya Thanki who provided us with very timely analysis and insight into the areas under discussion and raised some very pertinent questions for us to address. Much credit goes to Anil Advani and Gordon Peters, not only for their wisdom, their practical help, and their constant encouragement, but also for being there for us when most needed.

Finally, we are much indebted to Save the Children Alliance for their commitment to the issues raised in the book. Their help has made the publishing of this book possible.

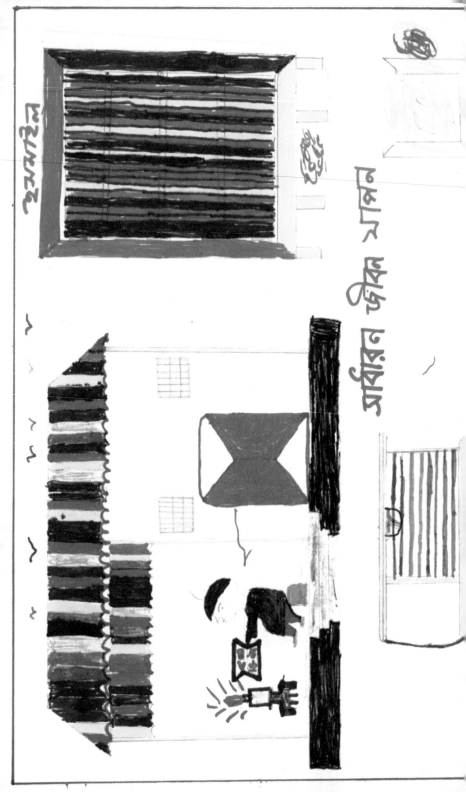

CHAPTER 1

INTRODUCTION

Perhaps to make the situation sound less brutal and to protect the sensibilities of the better off, people living in poverty have been described variously through the last few decades. From being "poor" to being "needy", "destitute", "deprived", "disadvantaged", they are now termed as 'people living below the poverty line'. No matter what terminology is used to refer to the people living in poverty, their reality does not change. Their lives, and those of their families, remain dehumanised by poverty.

Much has also been written about poverty—its causes and manifestations, its levels and its victims. Enormous effort, time, energy and resources from governments, non-government and private organisations and international institutions have gone into reducing poverty. But, it continues to persist, ever stronger and increasing. And in varying degrees it is all around us, no matter where we live, in rich or poor parts of the world. Some of us are able to see it for ourselves on our streets, in our neighbourhoods, in our cities, while others see it on TV or read reports and statistics about lack of food and shelter, about diabolical living conditions, about suffering and struggle of massive numbers of people near and afar. Within these struggling, suffering masses, are children striving to survive, largely without little means of survival—and clinging to the hope of a better tomorrow.

The living conditions of people whose existence is blighted by poverty display common features throughout the world: lack of sufficient food, less than basic or adequate shelter, no health care, few clothes, lack of clean water ... the list is endless. Only a few lucky ones get access to basic amenities, education and work. Lack of fair and adequate returns for their toil means people cannot break free of their poverty. The majority of such people live hand to mouth and are barely able to sustain themselves, let alone their families. Needless to say child poverty is mostly a direct consequence of adults living in poverty. In fact, generations of children are born and grow up in poverty, learning to fend for themselves and their families from a very early age.

In this book twelve urban children convey their reality of life of wants and a wish for a childhood without wants. These children happen to be from Bangladesh, yet they could be from favelas in Brazil or slums in Indonesia. Their living conditions and struggles are the same but their life stories different, their ambitions and aspirations individual and personal.

Bangladesh is amongst one of the poorest countries in the world. Poverty here is endemic and highly visible in cities and towns. Here, an estimated 20 million children live and grow up in conditions one can only describe as inhuman and soul-destroying. Poverty here is so visible that it surrounds you as soon as you step outside your home, and for the majority of Bangladeshis it surrounds them within. On the streets of Dhaka, the capital of Bangladesh, beggars with missing body parts, children emaciated with hunger and covered in dirt and pollution, women with a number of scrawny children in tow, ambush the passers-by for a few taka. Most of us avert our eyes as if by avoiding them we can wish away their existence. Perhaps acknowledging their presence means recognising our own role in perpetuating poverty. The daily confrontation with destitution and misery has made us immune to the pain and suffering of the needy. Many use ignoring the poor as a coping strategy for a problem so enormous that we know it will not go away with a few taka. Others give whatever they can to help. But many simply don't care as they genuinely believe that the poor are responsible for their own fate, that they are poor because they are lazy and would rather beg than work.

We are living in a world dominated by global economy and market system, markets flooded with consumer goods from home and abroad, and consumers being urged to buy newer and more tempting products constantly. Thus, even in Bangladesh, where half the population lives below the poverty line (defined by the World Bank and the United Nations as an individual living on less that one US dollar a day), amongst a certain class of people consumerism is rife, and the pressure to compete with the Alis rampant. The life-style of some is as opulent as, if not more than, many of those in rich countries.

Children living in poverty are not only sharply aware of the disparities between their lives and the lives of the better off, they also know very well what they miss out by not being born into rich families. A good deal is known about what children living in poverty are encumbered with; how many of them are literate or illiterate, how many work at what age, and so on. But there is scant knowledge about how they experience their poverty, what they feel about living on the margins of society, what are the issues that concern them, how they view the world they live in, and what their hopes and ambitions are.

The purpose of this study was to examine the following:

- What are the life experiences of these children living in a spiral of poverty?
- How soon in life do disparities between themselves and others become evident to them?
- What are their reactions, both emotionally and practically, to their impoverishment?
- What are their aspirations?
- With a major part of the population living in dire poverty how does this impact on society at large?

With the help of children living in slums of Dhaka, this book tries to answer the above and many other questions that pertain to the life chances for the majority of children in Bangladesh. Their views of what it means to be poor, and what it means to be rich, their present lives, their ambitions and their aspirations are recounted by them. This book is an attempt to allow the children surviving in poverty to describe their own conditions; to look at poverty and its impact from close quarters. The book is a testimony from the children who live lives marred by poverty.

This chapter gives a brief overview of the purpose of the book and the methodology used in compiling it. Chapter 2 describes the setting of the book by tracing the history of Bangladesh, and outlining the current situation of the country and of Dhaka, its capital, where the study was based. In Chapter 3 the children tell their stories in their own words. Out of the children's stories emerge themes that unite their lives in poverty. Each theme reflects how children's lives, self image and future are shaped by the world and its reactions towards the poor. The children's stories are interspersed with these themes, which provide the threads that are common to all the stories.

Chapter 4 concentrates on the views, thoughts and ideas on poverty, its causes and effects that emerged in the focus group discussion with

140 children between the ages of four to fifteen. Within the context of their existing situation, limited resources and non-existing support systems, the children describe a future for themselves. The children extend their vision to include their hopes for an equitable and just Bangladesh and a world where there is peace and where humanity prevails.

Chapter 5 relates the local with the global to show the connection between the impact of dominant international forces—be it the economic systems, the political agendas, or the ideology of 'me first'—on creation, exacerbation and experience of poverty locally. And the concluding chapter explores the actions that need to be taken globally by different players involved in poverty alleviation work—especially if they are truly committed to bringing about real changes in the lives of more than two billion people living in poverty round the world.

The book contains statistical data, as well as extracts from newspapers and magazines to support some of the points made by the children, and also to highlight the scale of problem that exists worldwide. Over all it is clear that these children or the 'poor' of the world are not a monolith. They are persons with rights who, each in their own way, try to survive in a world dominated by exploitation, materialism and competition.

We have refrained from using terms like developed/developing, First World/Third World, advanced countries, for these are value-laden definitions based on western concept. Instead we have employed the terms 'rich' or 'north' and 'poor' or 'south' countries/world, based simply on their economic status.

Methodology

The principal part of the material for the book comes from a) focus group discussions with children of various ages and b) in-depth interviews and discussions with twelve children and their parents/guardians living in Dhaka slums. All aspects of their existence, from housing, schooling, social networks, work (including domestic chores as well as paid work outside the home), to recreational activities have been looked into and discussed.

The complexity of poverty as well as the ages of the children necessitated an exploratory approach to understand how they view their lives and their futures. As the main aim of the study was to illustrate poverty as experienced by urban children, a primary school in Dhaka—

set up for children from the slums of the surrounding locality—was selected. This school was specifically chosen for four reasons:

1. It gave the authors access to children from the ages of 4 to 15 who had been in the education system.

2. Through its literacy class the authors were able to reach children who had had no previous access to education.

3. Previous research in the school by the authors had revealed that all of the children lived in slums in very deprived conditions.

4. The authors' existing relationship with the school meant that the children knew them and were comfortable enough to speak to them freely.

Besides holding focus group discussions (involving 140 children), in-depth interviews were conducted with ten children, representing those enduring the greatest level of impoverishment among those attending the school. To get an insight into the lives of children living on the streets, two street children were found through a non-government organisation (NGO) and were also interviewed. A general questionnaire was used as a guideline but children were allowed to narrate their stories freely. Interviews were also held with parents (except in the case of the street children) in their homes. All the discussions and the interviews were conducted in Bangla (taped) and transcribed in English by the authors with little or no editing.

At the onset, ethical issues of encroachment and privacy were of concern, and permission was sought from parents/guardians. However, once the interviews started it became evident that all involved, including the participants in the focus group discussions, were eager to talk about and share their circumstances with us and, more vitally, with the wider world. The participants wanted us to see and understand how they survived and managed in adverse conditions. Pseudonyms have been used for all the participants to protect their identity.

Outcome

The narratives, of both children and parents, reveal that life circumstances for each one of them are different. Of the twelve children interviewed, one actually lives on the street, while one, although categorised as living on the streets, has a shelter to go to (NGO), one lives with his grandparents, a few live in large extended families, one lives with his father while the mother continues to live in the village.

All, except the street children, live in the slums in one of the wealthiest parts of the city. Their homes are mainly patched together huts or tin shacks—the living space dire but clean. The surrounding areas are grim and squalid. Only two out of the ten homes have electricity. All have to fetch water from outside. Cooking is done outside the huts, and toilet and washing facilities are either open space or the pond. Of the twelve children, ten have migrated from rural areas, and within the city have had to move house more than once.

All the same, each child has something unique to divulge—their experience, dreams, ambitions, and aspirations. Whereas one girl dreams of being a singer as well as a doctor, another simply wants to be back with her parents. How they synthesise the world is also distinctive to each one. For example one 13-year-old told us that living in the city had taught him that without money there is no freedom. The depth of the insight these children possess with regard to their predicament is astonishing. A few of the working boys find their work hard, but are aware that without their earnings their families may have to go without food so they continue to toil. Some of their observations are startling— particularly in some of the younger age band. For example some four-year-old children told us that the poor need education so that they can do better for themselves. The children express how poverty continues through generations. It is clear that a number of the participants associate the poverty their grandparents lived in as a cause of their parents' and their own poor conditions. The account of their families' struggle to change their circumstances defies the fallacy that the poor are, or remain, poor due to their own fault. The children also show how wide their comprehension is of the world of the rich and display a deep understanding of how inequalities are perpetuated.

Despite the slim chance of breaking out of this cycle of deprivation, there is hope amongst the children and their parents of a better, though not necessarily wealthier, future. The children provide insights into the causes and the effects of poverty. They also present some solutions to their problems. Additionally, the authors put forward some further explanations of the causes and the impact of poverty from a socio-economic and a political perspective within Bangladesh, and in a global context and explore some steps that could be taken to reduce it.

Implications

We anticipate that some of the insights and challenges presented by the children will spark a debate and take the 'poverty alleviation/reduction programmes' to a level where they can make an impact on impoverishment in actual, concrete, reality. We also hope that this book might offer some preliminary practical trajectories for further studies.

The children's observations testify that without fundamental transformation in our thinking regarding rich-poor relations, those both between richer and poorer nations and between poor and affluent people, and radical changes (not reforms) in the economic and social systems, very little will be achieved in terms of poverty reduction. The numbers of people still living in poverty in Bangladesh (and the world over) proves that years of effort on the part of numerous agencies and organisations to alleviate poverty has achieved some but not fundamental changes. Our assertion is that the majority of government, as well as non government agencies, are chiefly guided by and operate within the existing and now globally accepted economic system i.e. capitalism, which we believe is not necessarily the best system for poverty reduction, leave alone eradication.

We expect the people who read this book to get a closer view, and thereby understanding, of the conditions of children living in poverty— their day-to-day life, their aspirations and hopes. The importance of the findings cannot be overstated, as the voices of the children represented here should provide both insights and challenges that the poverty alleviation programmes seek to address.

While the spotlight of the book has been on Bangladesh, the findings are equally valid for other poverty-stricken areas of the globe. Children living in poverty in other parts of the world, including the developed world, could easily identify, to a greater or lesser degree, with the feelings expressed and the issues raised by the children in Dhaka.

CHAPTER 2

BACKGROUND: BANGLADESH AND DHAKA

Poverty is without borders; it is widespread and deep-rooted. There are over two billion people considered as "poor" in this world. No matter how rich the nation, one can still find people living in poverty. It is estimated that in the US, the richest country on earth, 35.9 million people are classified as living below the poverty line.[1] The nature of poverty, its causes and effects are situational. To understand what it means to be poor, one must understand the context in which one is poor. Being poor in Sub-Saharan Africa will be different from being poor in America. The causes of poverty are both local and global. History, resources, policies and politics determine the extent of wealth and equitability in its distribution. National policies at times are dictated by global issues and agendas, totally out of the control of individual nations. It is the interplay between the local and the global which makes causes of poverty both the same and different, whether in Bangladesh or in Brazil. So why undertake an investigation into poverty in Bangladesh? Is it because Bangladesh at the present time is considered one of the poorest countries in the world? But so is Zambia. Is it because for three years running Bangladesh has been found to be the most corrupt country on earth? But many others are not far behind. Essentially the book is about children living in poverty, and not about any one nation. Since both the authors live and work in Bangladesh, the information for the book comes from here. All the same, some of the data collected could be equally valid for another country categorised as poor. But as stated earlier, it is the geopolitical situation of any country and its management of the interplay between the local and global that determine the living

---

[1] http://www.indymedia.ie/newswire.php?story_id=66352&time_posted_upper_limit=1093
665600&time_posted_lower_limit=1093579200.

conditions for its population. And Bangladesh has its own particularities that determine the economic, social and political status of its people.

A brief background of both Bangladesh and of Dhaka, where all the contributors to the book live, might be helpful to put the substance of the book in context. In this chapter, the authors look at Bangladesh, its history and experiences to understand the environment and its contribution to poverty creation and exacerbation. The physical description of Dhaka aims to give the readers a feel for what it is like to live in a city where traffic seems to increase by the hour and buildings sprout overnight.

For people round the world in general, Bangladesh conjures up the image of floods and mayhem at best, and at worst a poverty-stricken nation desperately in need of help. And in recent times, added to this is its infamy of being the most corrupt country on earth. It is true that Bangladesh is prone to floods, and it is also well known that corruption is a fact of life in the country. But it is poverty—in part caused by these two factors—that is visible and inescapable, particularly in the cities and towns.

History

Bangladesh has a rich but often traumatic history. Incursions (over two millennium) by Aryans, Moguls and Europeans resulted in peaks and troughs of peace and prosperity on one hand, and devastation and destitution on the other. The end of British colonisation of India in 1947 left in its wake a country split in two, the fault-line being religion. The predominantly Muslim regions in the east and the west of India formed a new country, Pakistan. But the two parts of this new country, East and West Pakistan, were separated by a thousand miles, and this spatial disconnection also represented the separation of languages, cultures, social and economic development as well as political aspirations. From 1952 onwards a struggle for autonomy ensued in East Pakistan, which peaked in the late 60s. After much bloodshed and loss of life, freedom was won in 1971, and the People's Republic of Bangladesh emerged as an independent country. But its troubles were not over yet.

The post-independence period, with no economy to speak of and a tattered infrastructure, was marked by frequent political in-fights and military coups. And as if all this was not enough, in 1973-74 the country experienced the most severe famine. It was not until 1991 that the parliamentary elections were held. Since then Bangladesh continues to operate as a democracy with, by and large, two main parties dominating the political scene: the Awami League and the Bangladesh National Party.

Once the wealthiest part of the sub-continent, globally famous for is muslin cloth and jute and jute products, Bangladesh today is counted amongst one of the poorest countries in the world, with almost half of its population living below the poverty line. Furthermore, the number of people living in poverty has increased during the 1990s, and like elsewhere in the world, since the '70s the gap between the rich and the poor has also grown.

The People

Notwithstanding the poverty, Bangladeshis are a hospitable, generous and proud people. Even the poorest of the poor will offer their visitor a bite to eat, or something to drink. The family plays a major role in people's lives even in urban areas. In the absence of any welfare system, generally the family provides what support it can to the more deprived of its clan. Patronage also plays an important part in an individual's survival and betterment, for Bangladesh remains a class-and status-riven society in which without patronage it is difficult to achieve the simplest things such as getting a job or admission into college. With patronage one can jump queues, bypass all equality considerations, rise to the highest levels, often without possessing skills or qualifications. Amidst corruption, inefficient systems and mind-boggling bureaucracy, the poor strive to make the best of a nearly hopeless situation. For not all poor are lazy or lacking in initiatives or ingenuity, just as not all rich are hard working or productive. Many of the rich in fact inherit their wealth, and many accumulate it, and not always through legitimate means.

The 133 million people are mainly Bengali with around a million comprising of various tribal groups, mostly living in the Chittagong Hill Tracts. The majority of the population is Muslim (87%). Hindus account for 12% of the inhabitants, and Buddhist and Christians make-up the remaining 1%. Eighty per cent of the population live in the countryside, which is lush green, beautiful and picturesque—but behind the pleasing scenery, for most, lurks hunger and deprivation which neither family support nor patronage can alleviate.

Major NGOs, foreign aid and government programmes have focused their efforts in the rural areas, dealing with education, health and, of course, poverty. Some noteworthy achievements have been made such as reduction in population growth, near self-sufficiency in food (people go without as they lack the purchasing power rather than any deficit in the market productivity), micro-credit systems, improvement in infant mortality rate, rise in literacy etc. But grinding poverty persists for many. Becoming landless through floods or being forced out of one's property by gangsters, losing all through debt, not finding gainful employment are not uncommon for the rural populace, forcing them to migrate to the cities.

The cities in Bangladesh are bursting at the seams with relentless population flowing into them. But the chaos and the uncontrolled development in the cities cannot be attributed to migration from rural areas alone. Other economic and political factors are responsible as well. But certainly the increase in the number of slums and the increase in the slum population is a direct result of people uprooting themselves from the villages. Like Mia, an 11-year-old boy, explains: "I would like to have a home in Dhaka after marriage, not in the village. In the village even when you work very hard you don't get enough to eat."

Now and Future

Post-independence development in Bangladesh for various reasons became heavily dependent on aid money and expertise from wealthy countries. This dependency unfortunately continues after 30 years and has skewed minds and relationships of people. It has also exacerbated the culture of corruption, patronage and class divisions. For it appears that where there is money, misappropriation follows quickly, making some very rich while others poorer. The divide between the have and have-nots has widened severely, poverty landlessness and unemployment have increased and income distribution is more unequal than ever.

For the poor the future looks bleak because redistribution of wealth or equal opportunities do not feature as a priority on the policy makers' agenda. But, as in most poor countries, modernisation, progress, development (read "catching up with the western world at any price"), are definitely on the agenda. The donors, the World Bank, the IMF and the country's elites, who also have a vested interest in pushing such a programme, exert a disproportionate influence on the state and veer it in a particular direction which may prove beneficial for some but not automatically for the majority of the people.

Bangladesh: At a Glance

Population	133 million (2003)
Population living below poverty line	50 per cent
Percentage of population between ages 0-15	40 per cent of the total population

Number of children working	8.3 million
Percentage of working children between the ages of 5 to 9	8.9%
Number of street children	4 million (this includes children who work on the streets but live at home as well as children actually living on the streets)
Malnutrition rate amongst children under 5	56%
Life expectancy	60.5
Female	60.9
Male	60.1
Literacy	41.4 (2002)
Female	35.6
Male	47.6
Rural	37.2
Urban	63.6
Income inequality	1995 poorest 5% earned 1.03% and the richest 5% 18.85% of the GNP
	2000 poorest 5% earned 0.88% of and the richest 5% 23.26% of the GNP

Dhaka

Dhaka, a city of 11 million people, is the opposite of the rural scenario of serenity and beauty where poverty is more or less hidden behind the tranquillity. Bangladesh is one of the most densely populated places in the world, and this is patently evident in Dhaka. Overcrowding and congestion (caused by humans as well as traffic) have denuded the city of most of its beauty, charm, lakes and green spaces. Dhaka offers its overflow of population little respite from noise, traffic and pollution. Public amenities of any kind are few and far between. Yet, Dhaka is in the throes of massive development—mainly apartment blocks and shopping plazas, further shrinking the green and open spaces, and leading to major infrastructural deficiencies. Amidst all this growth and development lie massive pockets of poverty. In this capital city of Bangladesh, poverty is very much "in your face." With the exception of some well-to-do areas and some government buildings, the condition of the city roads and buildings, the lack of basic amenities and the large number of beggars on the streets plainly tell the tale of paucity and hardship.

However, there is also evidence of wealth in the new apartment blocks with most modern designs and up-to-date facilities, in the plazas full of consumer goods (including the latest electrical goods and designer-label products) and in car showrooms where one can pick from the newest sports model on display—if one has the money).

In the last hundred years the city population has increased thirty-fold and it continues to grow at a rapid rate of five per cent a year. This is largely due to persistent migration from the rural areas with people escaping poverty, displacement, homelessness, persecution and discrimination (class, gender and religious). The majority of new arrivals do not have a place to live or jobs to go to. Slums or streets provide them abode and while many find life difficult—and often brutal—and the environment anything but pleasant, almost all prefer this to the lush green villages they left behind, as here at least they can, with or without a job, eke out a living.

> Every year around 300,000 people from rural areas arrive in Dhaka looking for work and survival. A substantial number of these are children on their own, who end up living and working on the streets of Dhaka.

According to the 1999 census of slums in Bangladesh, carried out by the Bangladesh Bureau of Statistics, dotted around Dhaka are 1,579 slums, some quite sizeable, housing 500 plus households, and some small with around 70 to 100 people. But some of the NGOs dispute this number and suggest that there are over 20,000 slums in the city. However, even if one works on the government figures, with roughly 200,000 households living in slums, the total estimate could be 1 million people. That is ten per cent of the population in Dhaka.

Dhaka draws adults and children alike. Most of the children who come alone into the city end up on the streets. A conservative estimate puts the number of street children (children living and working on the streets of Dhaka) at 50,000. Almost 80 per cent come from the rural areas. Approximately 10,000 girls are working (visibly) as prostitutes on the streets of Dhaka—many as young as 9 and the majority around 14 years of age. There are many thousands who work in hotels or brothels. While it is easy to assess the numbers of girls in the sex industry, it is difficult to work out how many boys are involved as, first they are not visibly obvious and second, they will not admit to this work. Only about ten per cent of the street children get helped by the Government agencies and the NGOs.

On a daily basis, thousands of people arrive in Dhaka with hopes and expectations. It is projected that by the year 2030 the population here will double to 22 million, making it a mega city. Already, constrained infrastructure, non-existent support systems, and the growing crime rate make survival difficult and risky. In this milieu live children whose survival and development is dependent upon decisions taken by others, decisions which the children or their parents cannot influence. The children in these stories describe what it means for them to live on the threshold of survival and how they see their future unfolding in these circumstances. They describe their hopes for themselves and their vision for the future of Bangladesh and the world.

CHAPTER 3

OUR STORIES AND OUR CONCERNS

This section presents children's stories as narrated by them. Themes that emerge from the stories and discussion are interspersed with these stories

Parveen

Parveen and I met at INCIDIN, an NGO that works with children living on the streets. Parveen had been briefed by the INCIDIN staff about the purpose of my meeting with her. We sat in a room at the INCIDIN centre. Although she was dressed in well-worn clothes, she looked neat and tidy. It was difficult to gauge her reactions to this meeting. There were no expressions on her face, or voice to indicate how she felt about talking to me about her life

Once I have started to do well, I will go home. I am waiting for that day. I wrote to my parents telling them I am OK and not to worry.

My name is Parveen. I am fifteen-years-old. I came to Dhaka nine months ago. A very deep [close] friend of mine told me that she would get me a better job in a garments factory here. I left the house without telling my parents. I thought I would tell my parents when I had started to do well for myself in Dhaka. My friend brought me to Dhaka and took me to a flat. There were two other women there and a child. The man who used to bring clients there also owned the place.

This is how I got into sex work. The friend must have gotten money out of this, otherwise why would she do something like this? The money that the men used to give was not given to me. I had no money.

My family lives in Babubazar. I have three brothers and three sisters. All my sisters are married. One is married to a shopkeeper, another to a bus driver, and the third one to a businessman. My elder brothers are working. One has a shop, and the other is in service. My youngest brother goes to school. I am the youngest in the family. My father has studied till Class VIII, and my mother till matriculation. My father has one *katha* of land on which he grows vegetables. It is land that has been passed on to him from his father. My mother is from Barisal.

I used to work in a garments factory when I was with my parents. I had worked there for nine months. I used to work from eight in the morning till ten at night. I used to be very tired by the time I got home. My parents would help me by getting me my food, washing my clothes etc. I had to work because it was becoming difficult to run the family otherwise. That is why I thought coming to Dhaka would help my family. I used to earn Tk 1850 per month in the factory. All the money I used to earn was given to my parents.

We had a tin house. It had wooden walls and a tin roof. We used to get water from the hand pump. There were shared *pukka* [concrete] latrines. There was electricity in my house, light, fan and a TV. There is a river close to my house. We used to bathe in the river.

I used to study in Class IV before I started working. It was a co-ed school. I used to enjoy school. I liked science and Bangla. I found math very difficult. It used to take me about 20 minutes to walk to the school. I used to study in the evenings to do my homework. When it was exam time, there was no play, only studying. My parents also used to stress that I should study and do well in the exams. I would like to resume my studies one day.

One day I escaped from the flat and came to the stadium. I started to sleep on the streets. I lived on the streets for three months. An apa [sister] from here [INCIDIN—an NGO that works with street children] told me about this place. So I decided to check this out. Now I do not do sex work at all. I am doing work for this place now. I tell other girls about this place. I tell them that if they want, their lives can change too. I get taka 500 per month for this work. I have to spend three months like this, without resorting to sex work, then I will be able to go to another centre. Here, at this present centre, I cannot spend the night. I go back to the streets at night. If I can stay away from sex work for three months, I will be promoted to another centre. There I will learn skills so that I can support myself.

I would like to learn how to sew. I want my own machine. So I will get my own work. Once I have started to do well, I will go home. I am waiting for that day. I wrote to my parents telling them I am OK and not to worry. I also got a reply from them. They said they wanted to see me and they wanted me to do well.

Life on the streets was and is very difficult. People say all kinds of things. They say bad things to you. It is still very difficult, but now because people know me they do not worry me too much. I know the guards and the mastaans [the local gangs], so they do not disturb me. When it rains, it is difficult to find a place to stay. People are small minded. They look down upon me because I am poor. I am poor, that is why this is happening to me.

I like to watch TV. We had a TV in our house. I liked movies which had action and fights in them. I never went to the cinema hall. I do not watch anything here at this centre. When I used to live at home, I knew everyone in the neighbourhood. We girls played together. We had a great time. Here it is different. There is no fixed schedule. Girls come in when they can get away, or when they need to. So there is no certainty that you will meet the same girls every day. We don't know each other. We all have different times. When I come in, some are sleeping, some have gone to have a bath or are eating. There are a few that I can talk to. I sometimes read storybooks, children's books. I can eat two meals on most days. On some days (2-3 times in a week), I cannot get two meals. I get angry when people abuse, or threaten me. I do not like fights.

One can progress in Dhaka. In the village one is ignorant—simple- minded. But, in Dhaka one learns very quickly. I want to stand on my own feet. I want to lead a normal life. For me the day I stand on my own feet will be the happiest day. I want to be like Laila Apa [a woman who works in INCIDIN]. I like the way she walks, the way she talks. She leads a normal life.

Parveen narrates her traumatic experience in a dispassionate voice. It is almost as if she is telling you something that happened not to her, but to another person. There is no anger against the friend who got her in this situation; no feelings of revenge come through when she is talking about her life. It is only when she is speaking of her own convictions and ambitions that one can see a spark of emotion. She speaks emphatically of her need to support herself and to "become something". She acknowledges the hard work that is ahead of her and the fact that she still has a while to go before she moves on to the centre for vocational training.

There are many questions unanswered about Parveen's life before she came to live on the streets. It does not seem that there was a crisis in the family that propelled her in this direction. Parveen's story highlights how vulnerability has different thresholds. In Parveen's case it seems a deterioration of living standards was the catalyst for her leaving school and joining the workforce. Today there is a quiet determination within her to make something of her life.

Ali

I would start at two in the afternoon and carry on till six and then have a break and start again and work till eight at night. In the morning I had to wake up early to go and get the balloons from the factory. Some days I just didn't do it. I really found it difficult. It was very hard. I used to get very upset and angry thinking I am so little, I should be in school, I should be living in a house, I should be with my mother. I should not be roaming from street to street without food or shelter, being kicked and abused by people.

Ali has been living on the streets for the last six years. Since the age of seven he has been separated from his mother, as after his father's death his mother was unable to support the two of them. Last year he was befriended by INCIDIN, a Dhaka-based organisation working with and for street children, and through their drop-in centre for street boys he has had health check-ups, counselling and a place to occasionally have a bath and wash clothes.

Ali is thin to the extent that all his bones show. But he is clean and dressed in reasonable clothes. He tells his story in a serious tone, but without much emotion. At one point, I breakdown listening to what he has to endure, and the child in him shows through, in need of love and affection. Yet he consoles me and philosophises about life and all that it bestows.

He is quite excited that I will tape his interview and throughout keeps an eye on the machine to ensure that it is working. In fact, at one point it goes off and only due to Ali's vigilance do I know that I need to push the plug in again. At the end of the interview I play back the tape and he is extremely pleased to hear his recorded voice.

My father died when I was little. My mother could not manage to keep us even though she worked. She has a machine at home and sews clothes for people. We did not have enough to eat. We have no other family; my grandparents on both sides are dead. Other relatives and friends are in no position to help us. I have one uncle [father's brother]; he has some money but he does not want to know us. After my father's death he has not bothered to see how we are managing. I came to Dhaka when I was seven. I came with a friend. He was 14 or so. We used to sell balloons. Now I have no work. This friend used to take a big amount of challan [commission] from me. If I earned 200 takas he would take 100. Then my friend started to ask me to do bad work [sex work]. He wanted to teach me and push me into this line. But I refused. He used to look after me when we first came to Dhaka. Now we have fallen apart.

I go to see my mother once every two months or so. I go just for the day. My mother wants me to stay in the village but there we can't eat. Here in

Dhaka I can still get some work, whatever, and manage. I always take he
some money. There are days when I have nothing to eat and some days
manage on little, but I would not get even that in the village. Sometime
someone asks me to give them a massage and I earn a little like that.

I have friends on the street. We are about 10 to 12 children in the patch
I live in. Some are the same age as me, some are older. Some don't have any
parents. Most have come from the village. We talk to each other and have
become friends. I have got to know them. I sleep in the doorway of a shop
Near me sleeps a girl; she is twelve-years-old.

I wake up and sometimes go to the centre [INCIDIN's drop-in centre] for
a bath, and also have breakfast there. Other times I don't bother. I use public
toilets. Then if I have money in my pocket I have something to eat, else I
manage without. When shops open, I go to the proprietors asking for work. I
go from shop to shop but get nothing. No one gives work without some
reference. Where can I get a reference from? Then I wander about a bit with
my friends, talk to them, spend time with them in the park or whatever. Then
it is night. Sometimes someone asks me to go home with them to give them a
massage. Other times nothing. I just go off to sleep.

I did not go to school in the village. I was doing some studies at home. Then
my father died. If he had been alive, I would have gone to school. I do not go
to any school in Dhaka.

In the village my mother has a small one-room mud hut with a little yard.
She cooks in the yard. There is electricity and water. We don't have a toilet;
we just go outdoors behind the hut. I want to save money and do business, but
I do not have enough to eat so how can I save for a business? I want to set up
a little shop. My father used to drive an auto rickshaw. If he were alive we
would have been OK.

I am poor. I have nothing. We have just the little house in the village. My
mother has to do sewing work to survive. Despite her efforts we still don't
manage to make enough to eat properly. We are poor; we have nothing. My
father's death has made us poor. If he had been around life would have been
different.

When I was earning, half my money went to my friend. He probably gave
some to the police. I was too young. I just gave the money I was asked. I did
not like selling balloons. I had to roam the streets the whole day long. I would
start at two in the afternoon and carry on till six, and then have a break and
start again and work till eight at night. In the morning, I had to wake up early
to go and get the balloons from the factory. Some days I just didn't do it. I really
found it difficult. It was very hard. I used to get very upset and angry thinking

I am so little, I should be in school, I should be living in a house, I should be with my mother. I should not be roaming from street to street without food or shelter, being kicked and abused by people.

People do look down on us poor; they do not recognise us as human beings. The police harass us the most, day and night. They beat us, kick us, wake us up and take us to the police station. They won't say what wrong we have done. There are people who are doing really bad things, but the police don't say anything to them, they do not catch them. Us they beat up. Police are really bad; they beat up the good people without reason, and do nothing to the wrongdoers.

Six years of life on the streets—there is nothing I like about it. It is hard and difficult and full of disappointment. I hope someone will give me work but it does not happen. There are people who try to push us into bad [sex] work. I resist but they take me and make me do bad work. Many of the other children are in the same position. I don't mix too much with all the children in my patch. They talk about bad things. But I have one special friend.

In the village wealthy people behave badly towards us; they see us as low people, they don't like us. In Dhaka it is the same. We want to do good work and they make us do bad work. Rich people shoo poor people away. My one and only fear of living on the streets is being taken by the police, being locked up in the jail and beaten by them. If I become ill or something I can always go to the centre. I do want to live with my mother, be looked after by her, fed by her but what can we do, we are poor. I want to get a job and support her but I can't find any work. What can I do? I go for Eid to my mother. I go one day before and stay for two-three days. If I have money I take clothes and food for my mother. There I go for namaz [prayers], we have Eid food. My mother is one person I really look up to.

I want to do business or get a job. I do want to get married when I am about twenty. I want to marry someone who is good natured and well behaved—someone with some education. I want to live somewhere in peace. I have a friend who really likes me very much. She is 18-years-old and has a house. She has everything. She takes me to her house and feeds me. She treats me very well. I say to her "I live on the streets, I have nothing. Then why do you look after me?" She says that she likes me, just likes me. I would like to have just one child, a boy. I will educate my child, will make him a good person. I have become bad but I will not let my son do the same. I want to help him so that he can make his life. It's not good to marry early. They say it on the TV that it is not good to marry before you are 18. They say on TV that 25 or 26 *is a better age. I see TV sometimes standing outside the TV shop and sometimes in someone's house where I do massage.*

I want to some business in Bangladesh and after making some money I want to go abroad. I want to go to Singapore. I like Singapore. The people are nice there. There are nice places and it's pleasant to walk on the streets. In the village someone had gone and lived in Singapore. He told us about it. He said it is a fun place. You can see much. So I decided I will go there some day. I would like to earn money. This is my hope. I can make it with a good job. I don't want to do bad work.

The thing that upsets me most, makes me very unhappy, is that I have to live on the street. I have to put up with mean behaviour of people. People keep giving me hope of work but do not actually do it. They say to me come with me I'll give you work but make me do bad work. I have been in Dhaka six years and not a day of happiness, only hardship. I have seen children ruin their life with drugs. I don't do drugs.

If I get a good job and make my life I'll be happy.

If someone does not talk to me properly I get very angry, I get hurt.

My dream is to get a good job one day and be a big person and make my mother's life better

Life has been cruel to thirteen year-old Ali. At an age when he should have been protected, cared for and given love and affection, he was living and working on the streets of Dhaka. The last six years of living on and roaming the streets, pleading for work wherever and taking on whatever have been a real lesson in vulnerability for Ali. Police harassment, pressure from pimps and criminals to take on work that Ali does not want to do, demands from individuals who pick up Ali for one thing e.g. massage but coax him into doing "bad work," being derided by the better-off are elements that even now make Ali unhappy and cause him distress.

Ali is acutely aware that his existence and his mother's have been shaped by his father's death. With the father around, even though they were poor, there was protection, there was family life. Although it is always tempting for Ali to be back with his mother, it would literally mean starvation, so he carries on sleeping, eating, working on the streets of Dhaka. Although he lives in a group and there is an element of care for each other, in the final analysis it is each for oneself.

But human resilience comes through. Ali hopes, aspires and plans for the future like any of us. He wants to set up a little business or get a job and make his mother's life better. He wants to travel and meet people. And he wants to be seen as a human being and loved.

Life on the Streets

A conservative estimate puts the number of street children (children living and working on the streets of Dhaka) at 50,000. Almost 80 per cent come from the rural areas. Some of the children arrive in Dhaka at an early age of one or two with their families. When things get tough (problems with finding work, shelter) often the fathers leave the family with the mother to fend for the children. Such situations often lead to total destitution of life on the streets with children begging or collecting bits from the rubbish heaps and the likes to survive and support the rest of the family. In such situations some mothers are known to have abandoned their children to the benevolence of their fate.

The majority of girls living on the streets have been lured or forced by pimps or relatives or someone they know into coming to the city and becoming sex workers.

Many of the street children have some contact with their mothers but hardly any with their fathers. The children mostly live in gangs with an older one guiding and protecting but also taking a cut in earnings and often pushing children into criminal activities. But more often than not it is a pimp or a broker who controls a group, or groups, and directs their life and work.

The children sleep in stations, docks, parks and any place that will offer them shelter. Police harassment and brutality is not uncommon. These children are vulnerable and much at risk of being coerced or cajoled into criminal activities, begging or prostitution. They are easy targets for recruitment by criminals and for economic and political exploitation.

How Children Experience Poverty

Besides the obvious chasm in material existence, if one were to look for the one thing that distinguishes the "haves" from the "have-nots," it would have to be control over life. Children in these stories describe how little control they, or their kin, have over events that transpire in their lives. Where they live, at what age and kind of work they have to do, whether they can go to school, when they can study, and whether they can realise their ambitions are all dependent upon situations that they do not control.

> "I did not go to school, as money was needed for other things."
> — Rahman

From the time they can recall, they and their families have been dictated the course to be followed for survival. Bilal provides an insight into this when he says, "Living in the city I have realised there is little freedom without money."

The move from the village to the city, which the majority of the children have experienced, was dictated by circumstances beyond their control. Once the families arrive in Dhaka, the instability continues. Many children share their experiences of being evicted from their homes, either by individuals or by government agencies. The process

> "Before this we used to live in Kali Ghat. We were evacuated from there because the government started to construct houses there."
> — Farida

of eviction was a terrorising experience for some. They describe the physical demolition of their homes, or being evicted under duress, with trepidation that continues long after the process is over. As the threat of being forced out of their homes is ever present, the fear of having to move again stays with the children. They also voice their anxieties about being unable to find another house, or of having to move back to the village.

Parental unemployment and illness in the family are some of the other common causes of instability. Cost of illness tends to be higher for the poor in more than one way. Not only is the ill person's contribution to the family lost, but also money has to be borrowed, as there are hardly any savings for such events. When one is living hand to mouth, illness, accidents and the like invariably lead to debt, which inevitably contributes to further poverty. Ali's life is an obvious example of what happens to children from poor families when the main breadwinner is no more. Other children are aware of what might happen to them and voice their fear of losing their parents and the consequent uncertain future. Ahmed tells us, "I am scared of losing my parents. What will happen to me and my brothers and sister then?"

Living in poverty for the children, as for their parents, means day-to-day survival. It means residing in cramped, rough spaces with no basic amenities and foregoing food

> We eat two meals a day. Sometimes my mother is given food where she works and brings it home. Sometimes we do not have sufficient food to eat and go partially hungry.
> — *Zohra*

and pleasures. But added to these are the traumas and insecurities of, for example, having to move house, not knowing where the next "home" will be. Poverty also means not having enough to eat. Many children remark upon the snack received at school they attend as something they really appreciate because for some it is the first meal of the day. The

> The food industry spends around $40 billion annually on adverts aimed at wooing children world-wide to consume their products.

children who live on the streets indicate that they have to go without food for a couple of days in a week. The majority of children survive on two basic meals a day. Most days the meal consists of vegetable and rice as fish, meat and poultry are well beyond the reach of their families.

> Sakina Begum is amongst hundreds of the poorest in Dhaka City who has to forage for food for herself and her three children. In the nooks and crannies of this "concrete jungle" she searches for anything edible including leaves, flowers and grass. The money she makes from begging is not sufficient to buy even rice for the day.
> — *The Daily Star, 5/10/03*

Hunger affects the children's ability to learn; it affects their attention spans. Studies suggest that children who come from households with food scarcity show more learning and behavioural problems. Even marginal food insecurity can affect children's ability to learn.[2]

Related to food insecurity is the widespread malnutrition in Bangladesh. Children who were involved in this study looked smaller than their years. Research shows that a high proportion of children in Bangladesh are stunted. It is estimated that 700 people die of malnutrition-related causes every day in the country.[3] Malnutrition and inadequate intake of food, along with poor sanitation and hygiene, increase the incidence of disease amongst the children. Nutritional status also affects the children's ability to learn. Malnutrition is an ever-present fact of life for poor children, and

2 http://www.pediatrics.org/cgi/content/full/1081/44.

3 http://web.worldbank.org/WBSITE/EXTERNAL/NEWS/.

its effects have been well documented by various organisations. Girls, however, fare worst over all. Studies have shown that malnutrition at an early age has a long-term impact on girls as well as any children they have in the future.

Poor nutritional status at birth and low nutritional intake puts a vast number of children at a multiple disadvantage. They start their lives with odds heavily stacked against them. The families that they are born in are so involved in their struggle to survive that they are unable to provide the time, money, and other resources that would offset some of these odds and give the children a chance to realise their potential.

Being poor also means living in dirt and squalor. Children resent the conditions they live in. They recognise that poverty means living without basic amenities like running water, toilets and a sanitary and clean environment. They express a wish to live in better surroundings, where rubbish is not strewn around and where neighbours are committed to keeping their locality clean and tidy. When the children describe the houses they would like to live in, they do not plan on grand big houses. They simply desire cleanliness, peace, and basic facilities in their home and in their locale.

One can visibly sense the stress caused by poverty on these young children. Many of the children are pushed into early adulthood out of the need

> Ali, the boy living on the streets since he was seven, says that when he goes to meet his mother in the village he "always take her some money."

for survival. A strong sense of responsibility towards the family builds up from a very tender age. Some working children report their pride in contributing towards the family income. Others suggest they worry about where the next meal will come from and even though they find it hard, the children continue to work because they know that their income makes a difference to the family; without it survival would be at stake. Signs of untimely maturity are also evident because of the issues that the children have to face and deal with. Zohra when talking about her future says,

> I do not wish to marry now or when I am 25. But marriage will happen. As I grow older, if I am not married people will say, "The girl is so big and they are not getting her married." But how can one get married without meeting the demands [of dowry]?

Children—both those who do unpaid work at home and those who do paid work elsewhere—describe long and strenuous hours. The work at home involves, cleaning, cooking and looking after younger siblings. In between all of this is they manage to find the time to study and also to play a little. It would seem that children in poverty begin

> In 1995-96 close to 7 million children in Bangladesh, in the age group 5-14 years, were estimated to be economically active (including paid and unpaid work). This is approximately 19% of the total population in this age group.
> — *Bangladesh Bureau of Statistics*

multi-tasking at a very early age. Working for a wage starts early for many children. Most of them find their jobs hard and do not always like the work (or aspects of it). The children describe long working hours, often into the night, which they find physically exhausting. Bilal says that he does not like selling balloons but has to do so to get food. Amina, who works as paid domestic help, tells us about how she fears cleaning fans because it means climbing on the stepladder; or how she hates washing clothes in the winter. Yet they balance this with their schoolwork. But this balancing act must cause some pressure for the children. Studies on this issue have documented the presence of tension-related diseases such as anxiety attacks, headaches and acidity amongst working children.

Poverty might also be a cause of the shift in the traditional relationship between parents and children, where children become the caregivers. Children from a young age, both girls and boys, assume household responsibilities when their parents work outside. Younger siblings are often left in the care of the older ones. Housework is one of the main reasons cited by the children attending literacy class for opting out of regular school. It is estimated that 20 per cent of children of school-going age are not enrolled in schools. Most of these children are from poor and non-literate families.

At least for a few, it seems, a collaborative relationship with the parents emerges out of this struggle for survival. Ahmed shares how his father "advised" him to join a savings association. On the other hand, the very struggle for survival and living in uncertainty must cause stress in family relationships. However, not many children remark upon this.

Some children, like Ahmed, have control over the money they earn. For most, the earnings are handed over to the parents. They might keep a bit necessary for school or food, but most of it goes to the parents. Signs of maturity are clear from how children manage their resources. At an age when his better-off peers would save for toys etc., Ahmed is saving for a new house. But often money saved by the children gets clawed back by parents in a crisis situation. Zohra handed over her savings (she had made from the bit of money she got from her parents), to her father when money was needed for food. In fact less than half the children interviewed receive pocket money—those who do learn to save it. Others are reluctant to ask as they know their families' situation. But lack of it means you watch some children after school, or otherwise indulging themselves with treats, snacks, toys etc. Small and rare as these may be for others, for someone who just does not know what it is to have something extra, something special, a little personal fund could mean the world.

A strong family feeling comes through from some of the children's stories. A sibling who takes on more household work so that the school-going brother can study well, or the welcome that Amina gets from her siblings on her arrival on the weekends, indicates that some families at least are able to face adversity together. While some families are able to stick together, others are torn apart by poverty. Many children, due to pressures of poverty, have to live away from their parents. Stories narrated by Ali, who left his family back in the village to earn some money, or Shahin, whose brother had to go back to the village to earn something, show how poverty can uproot children (as well as adults) again and again in search for a living.

Such separation at an early age is a distressing experience for the children. Ali would much rather live with his mother in the village than be destitute on the streets of Dhaka. His mother also wants the same, but both know that this would mean starvation. Bilal and his father are also unhappy for having to live apart from his mother, but as the father says, "I feel bad living alone but what choice does a poor person have?" Living with relatives or strangers could be a difficult experience. Amina is lucky that her employer takes good care of her and supports her education through the literacy class. Not all domestic help are so lucky. Reports on the traumatic experiences of domestic help are commonplace. However, even when Amina stays with a sympathetic and caring woman, her dream is to live with her parents and brothers and sisters.

Socially defined gender roles, although continuing to exist, seem to get a bit blurred when survival is at stake. Children report that in case of severe poverty, rules are relaxed and women can do non-traditional jobs, like being a guard or a snack seller. These deviations are visible in the children's own lives also. Mothers go out of the house to work; unemployed fathers stay at home to look after the family. Or, working hours get organised to ensure at least one parent is at home, available for the children. Both boys and girls help in household chores, although girls report more work. Some jobs, such as cooking and washing utensils or clothes, generally continue to be off-limits for the boys, especially if there is a female in the household.

Poverty increases children's proximity to dangerous situations. Some children report having witnessed violent events and talk about criminal

> "We all hear news of kidnapping children everyday. The abducted children are sold in different countries for different uses. We have heard that the children are used in some countries for camel races. The louder the child cries, the faster the camel runs. Kidnapping kills so many dreams and lives."
>
> — *Momina, age 12*

activities in their locality. Most parents, however, continue to retain their traditional role of looking after their children as well as they can. Parents prepare their children to stay away from dangerous situations. Children say they are warned to look out for bad elements in society. They are aware of dangers of addiction and of those who might encourage them towards drugs.

> A survey carried out by Action Against Trafficking and Exploitation of Children (ATSEC) Bangladesh Chapter found that around 51 per cent of the victims of human trafficking are children between the ages of 11 to 18. Poverty and ignorance are the two main causes that lead so many to fall prey to pimps and brokers. Panch Bibi was taken into custody for smuggling 500 teenage girls in two years from the north of the country. The girls and their families had been promised well-paid jobs in Dhaka. Some of them of course may have ended up in Dhaka's brothels or hotels (a growth industry), but many such girls, and boys too, are shunted to India or the Middle East and forced into the sex trade, camel jockeying (mainly boys), and domestic work. Many are also trapped into selling body parts.
>
> Of the 406 participants in the survey, 52 per cent were found to be illiterate, and 81% from the poor class.
>
> — *The Daily Star 1/9/03*

Parents also worry about their children's present and future. Despite the need for money, Amina's mother is quite prepared to forgo Amina's monthly wage and bring her home so that she can study than let her work in a home where the employers may not permit her to continue schooling.

The need for education and the need to work co-exist. The children realise that they need to do both, and they manage their studies in the limited time they have after they have completed their household chores or other work. This in fact often means studying at night in the light of a lamp. The level of poverty is such that many cannot even afford a hurricane lamp. Many children mentioned the lack of materials such as books, notebooks, pens, pencils, tables and chairs required for doing their studies. The children value the support they get from their siblings or other members of the family, either in the form of direct help with studies or indirectly by freeing their time from other responsibilities. Peace and quiet, whenever available, are much appreciated as they allow the children to get on with their homework. Getting children educated requires much sacrifice from the parents and hardships for the children. Many, for example, have to walk to school for between 20 to 40 minutes (one way) and face not only daunting traffic but also inclement weather with temperatures rising to 38 degrees centigrade in summer and torrential rains and winds during monsoons.

To receive respect is a basic human need, but it cannot be taken for granted if one is poor. Children, especially girls, are offended by derogatory remarks made by others. They

> "When Auntie respects me, I forget I am poor."
> — Amina

worry that others will say bad things about them. Children remark upon the hurt they feel when the "rich don't look at the poor." Zohra says that she does not like to play with rich children, as they do not invite her to their house to watch TV. Respect by others, especially by the rich, could even compensate for the lack of wealth. Many children say they appreciate adults showing an interest in what they are doing. In fact the respect shown by village people to children from the cities is much remarked upon.

> A study, carried out in Britain amongst people experiencing poverty, suggests that the respondents wanted to be valued for what they were, and not who they were. In other words the need for respect is high on their list. They argued that although they did not have money to buy all that it can, they felt rich in other ways.
>
> — New Internationalist, 1999

Within these severe constraints, children are able to experience joy and celebrations. Whatever is available is made good use of. Games, which can be played with limited equipment,

> We couldn't do much for Eid. What can we do we did not even have *shemai*. No money so we all just stayed at home.
> — Zohra

bring fun into their lives. Lack of
resources can also be a source of
inspiration as Ahmed and his friends
show. Sharing the little that is
available they are able to buy

> For Eid I was selling balloons. At
> that time the sale goes up so no
> holiday for me.
>
> — *Bilal*

equipment for sports. They take sharing a step further by ensuring each
one of them is involved in caring for the equipment. But even some
major festivals such as Eid go unmarked as they are either working or
simply have no resources for festivity.

> One of the major festivals in the Muslin world is Eid. It follows a month of
> fasting and preparing for the final day itself, including frenzied shopping, for
> glamorous clothes and shoes (for men and women), jewellery, gifts and food,
> continues for days. But many children do not have the time or money to
> participate in the fun and joy of Eid celebrations. While sections of the
> community will have a 3-4 days holiday, which they will spend visiting family
> and friends, in their new shiny clothes, exchanging gifts and enjoying rich Eid
> food, many of the children (and adults as well) will be working away to make
> life pleasurable for the rest and eke out a living for self and family. Thousands
> of children like Rubel, working as domestic servants, will probably have to
> work harder on Eid with extra food preparation and cleaning. Yet, they may
> be luckier than many working in other spheres, for they will perhaps receive
> gifts, food and possibly even money.
>
> Shohag, for instance will spend the Eid day scouring the pans at a
> restaurant. He will receive a pittance for his backbreaking work. But when
> one is on the breadline, every taka matters. For Eid he would like to buy
> sandals and a shirt but knows that the money he earns is acutely needed at
> home. His father, a rickshaw puller, is doing his best to improve their lives
> but little Shohag has to supplement the income (even on Eid day) somehow
> (picking rags, breaking bricks, cleaning pots in restaurants). As Sohel says "Eid
> is nothing without money."
>
> — *The Daily Star, 29/11/02*

Poverty, for the majority of the people living in it, is unyielding, grinding
them down and leaving them without confidence or self-esteem.

All the children we spoke to feel their poverty acutely. For them it is
something tangible and experienced daily. At the same time it is not
about "I have this and I want more or better or something else." It's
simply about having little or nothing, about hunger, and degradation, of
living on charity and handouts, about back-breaking work and little
returns, about being ignored by the better off; about not having a voice,
about being marginalised and becoming invisible.

Tormented by poverty, a mother killed her two small daughters with pesticide and then attempted to take her own life. Dukhimon Begum Shahana, wife of a rickshaw van puller, was saved by the efforts of hospital doctors but begged to be allowed to die. "Why do you want to save my life? I do not want to live ... We do not have food and clothing .... Why should we lead such a life?"

— *The Daily Star, 24/7/03*

Ironically "Dukhimon" when translated means "unhappy heart." And there are hundred and thousands of *Dukhimons* across the world unable to feed and clothe their children.

Farida

I would like to marry a person who speaks well to women, does not fight, has a good job in an office.

Farida was part of the literacy class organised for children who had never been to school. She had been part of the literacy classes for a few months when I met her. She looked older than all the other students in her class. At the time of the interview, Farida was wearing a shabby, but clean, salwar kameez. She seemed a bit anxious about the meeting, but soon settled down to talk about her life and her dreams for herself and her family. She happily escorted me to her home on another occasion. Her family were obviously worried about the father who was unable to move due to a swelling around his stomach. Most of the conversations centred around the father's illness and around the insecurity of the lives of the poor.

I, Farida Akhtar, am twelve-years-old. I am enrolled in the literacy class at the school for poor children. I have four brothers and four sisters. My father, my mother, brothers and sister-in- law, all live in the same house. My father is sick, he has a swollen abdomen—panir rog. My brother pulls a rickshaw. My sister-in-law works in a garments factory. She goes at 7 AM in the morning and is back by 8 PM. My mother works in someone's house. She goes at ten in the morning and is back by 4 PM. All my sisters are married. They all live in Dhaka. None of my sisters are educated. My eldest brother has passed Class V or VI. My sister-in-law has also studied till Class V. My three younger brothers are in the same school as me.

My family moved from the village in Faridpur about 30 years ago. We don't go back very often. I have been to the village only two times. I live in a Bosti in Gulshan-2 with my family. We have been living in this area for the past seven-eight years. Before this we used to live in Kali … Zinzira Sadar Ghat. We were evacuated from there because the government started to construct houses there.

My house is made of cardboard and has a plastic roof. It is on the banks of the lake in Gulshan. We bathe in the lake. We use a wood-fired stove for cooking. There is no separate place for cooking. There is no latrine. But I can study in the house. I like that. There is a toilet in the area; there is also space to play in. I can also study well in this house. I would like to have a toilet, water, bathroom, more space, and a rubbish disposal drum in the house. I do not like the rain as the house is too flimsy. We eat rice, dal, fish, meat, eggs, vegetables. I like shutki bhartha (a dish made of dried fish).

People who live in this area are nice. They appreciate it if I greet them and show respect towards them. I do not like fighting. I do not like violence.

I have friends, both girls and boys. We play games like house-house, hopscotch, blindfold, skipping rope. We play together. We play ludo, carom board. Some of my friends go to school, others do not. They are all of the same religion.

I like studying. I like the fact that the school teaches us how to respect elders and treat them well. I like everything about the school—there is nothing I do not like. It is difficult for me to come to school. It takes 30 minutes for me to walk to school. English is difficult. But, students help each other. I can do the homework. But I find it difficult to write without seeing— "Na dekhe likha kathin." My family helps me to study. They get food for me, sometimes even by borrowing if needed. Or, by taking loans. My parents tell me to study well. My parents want me to pass, to do well in school, listen to elders.

The teacher teaches so many things. He teaches us Bangla, Maths, ABCD. I need many things to do well. I need books, pencil, rubber, notebook, chair, table and reading material to do well.

I help in the house. I clean, I do marketing. My sister-in-law helps in cleaning as well. I can cook too. When my sister-in-law is not there, my brothers also help. I would like to work in another house, do cleaning work, or look after the children, but it is difficult to get work. I am told to work first and then play. I am not allowed to go out alone, but have to go with my brother or some elder. I go with my mother to the bazaar and to the village.

I fear that our house might be broken, or set on fire by the government. I do not like it when people say bad things—"log kotha bole." There are some bad people also. Those who fight, "mauka mauki kore" are bad people. Women who wear make-up and those who see TV, songs and dance on the TV can become bad also.

We went to my sister's house for Eid. From there we went to the airport where we saw planes, helicopters, shops and lots of people. We ate food, especially sevain (vermicelli pudding with milk and sugar).

When I grow up I would like to work in a garments factory. I would like to marry a person who speaks well to women. Someone who does not fight. He should have a good job in an office. I would like just one child (no reason, just like that). I would like a boy, because boys work outside the house, whereas girls work at home. Afer marriage, I would like to stay in a rented place, not in the bosti as there is too much fighting and too many thefts.

I admire my cousin Sohel. He does not fight, has good character. He works in Wonderland where he has a shop. He is fourteen-years-old. I like Morsheda. She studies here in Class II in my school. She studies, works at home and has good chal chalon (character).

Farida's house is in one of the slums on the banks of the lake between Gulshan and Banani. Set on a small plot of land, the house has more space and privacy than other houses. The house is at the far end of the plot, almost touching the wall of a high-rise plush apartment building. Fatema's family was asked to live there on request of the landlord, who wanted someone to keep an eye on his property. There is a small veranda with a few chairs, a rectangular room at the back. Cooking is done outside the house.

Farida's father said that if they had to move out of this home they would move back to the village.

The family also has a small teashop where they sell some biscuits and a few grocery items. The elder brother has a rickshaw, which was given to him as dowry at the time of his marriage. But the rickshaw is broken and lying unused as it does not have a licence number.

Farida's mother works as house help. When she was asked whether her daughter-in-law liked to work in the garment factory she said, "Does she have a choice? For the poor it is not likes or dislikes that decide what they do."

Farida's father has been unwell for many years. He has a tumour that is protruding from his stomach. The tumour prevents him from undertaking many activities. He is unable to undertake trips into the city as the pollution makes him cough, and the resulting pain in the stomach is unbearable for him. He knows he needs to be operated upon, but is unable to find the resources to do so.

Farida is amongst the two million children in the country who had to forgo formal schooling. Children, particularly girls, are often called in to help in the house when others have more marketable skills. Once they have passed the age of enrolment into a primary school, there are few opportunities for learning to read and write. Non-formal literacy classes are mostly for adults, that too mainly in rural areas. The curriculum for adults is not readily applicable for children.

Farida echoes the insecurities many urban poor face—that of living in unauthorised slums in the city. Having seen her earlier home destroyed, she is constantly worried about a similar fate in her current home. There are more than 3,000 slums in Dhaka, of which only about one-fifth are authorised. Inadequate planning and resources as well as general apathy characterise urban planning in the country. Most families live in the slums without adequate access to sanitation, water and housing.

Living Conditions

According to the 1999 census of slums in Bangladesh, carried out by the Bangladesh Bureau of Statistics, dotted around Dhaka are 1579 slums, some quite sizeable, housing 500 plus households and some small with around 70 to a 100 people. But *The Daily Star* (TDS, 25/6/03) contends that roughly 2 million people now live in over 3,000 slums spread across Dhaka in "seriously unhygienic conditions." That is around 20% of Dhaka population.

I fear that our house might be broken, or set fire to by the government. I do not like it when people say bad things. I do not like the rain as the house is too flimsy.

— *Farida*

Farida's statement not only encapsulates the physical conditions poor children exist in but also gives an indication of the qualms they live with. Even something such as rain—a much awaited happening in hot countries—creates pangs of anxiety for Fatima. Her experience also has made her mistrustful of all officials. Other children also express their worries and concerns about their surroundings and living conditions, and it becomes clear that the long-term effects of existing in such deprived settings and internalising frustrations and fears cannot be positive for the individual or the population as a whole.

Except for two, who live on the city streets, all others interviewed live in the slums of Gulshan Thana in north Dhaka. Some of the slums are quite small in size, with around twelve families residing in an enclave while others house as many as 500 families.

Gulshan Thana in north Dhaka (comprising of three localities) is one of the richest areas in the city. Within its boundary are almost all the high commissions, embassies and consulates. The area also offers western-style supermarkets, malls and plazas, as well as consumer goods from all parts of the world for its wealthy and powerful residents (including foreigners, the majority of whom also live in this area). Nonetheless, the Bangladesh Bureau of Statistics (BBS) survey shows that Gulshan is not exempt from slums either. In fact the second highest number of slums (159 according to the BBS), are located in Gulshan.

The majority of the children residing in slums live in a one-room dwelling, with cooking and all other amenities outside the house. The rooms are generally

around 7'x 7' or 9'x 9' in size, except one which is double. Washing and toilet facilities are outside. Most do their cooking on wood fire. But two have kitchen facilities (also outside) with gas burners, which are shared by other families.

> We live in one room. We have no electricity or running water in the house. The toilet is by the lake—it is a partition—bath is done in the lake. Many people use this toilet.
>
> — Bilal

It appears that lack of privacy and overcrowding are something poor people simply live with. How this phenomenon affects children emotionally is difficult to say. Often as many as eleven people share a cell. Like accommodation, and a family of seven seems to be the norm in the slums. Yet, the fact is that while the children have remonstrated about the crowded conditions outside their home, nothing was said about lack of space within the house. This is most striking as one would expect that young girls and women would need some private space, especially in a culture where the concept of "modesty" is quite defined for women. Poverty, on the face of it at least, seems to blur proscribed rules and expectations.

Although these people live in a city, their living conditions, more than often, turn out to be worse than what they had in the villages. Hardly any have the benefits of utilities such as electricity, gas or tap water in the house, which most city dwellers take for granted. Only two of the ten interviewed have electricity in their homes. All have to fetch water from outside, mainly from tube-wells with pumps situated at 2-5 minutes walking distance. Cooking fuel for the majority is wood, burnt in mud stoves. Toilets are either in the open, or a hole in the ground within a cubicle of straw matting. Bathing and washing clothes are done at the tube-well. (Baths are taken with clothes on.)

A survey conducted (by the authors of this book) in 2002 into the living conditions of 104 children living in slums showed that almost all lived in similar circumstances and surroundings as the children in the book.

Energy

Around 2.5 billion people in the world have to live without gas or electricity. For their basic needs they use wood, crop waste and animal dung as fuel for heat and cooking. This is the second biggest killer after dirty water. "The smoke from their fires contains a cocktail of poisonous chemicals, which swirls around their homes, killing more than two million people a year—half of them children under five."

— Lean, 2002

> ### · Water
>
> In the developing world 2.2 million people die from drinking contaminated water–most of them children. Roughly 1.2 billion people do not have safe, clean water to drink and around 2.4 billion do not have adequate sanitation, leading to diarrhoea and other diseases and leaving people weak and unable to work or grow food for themselves.

Slum Population Profile: Bangladesh Bureau of Statistics, 1999

The vast majority of slum population are migrants who have moved to the city for survival

42% are below the age of 15

5% are unemployed

The bulk live in cell-like tin sheds or hutments, often without windows or ventilators

Amenities

44% have electricity

38% get water from tube-wells, 32% from taps, 3% from ponds or rivers

58% have makeshift toilets, 5% have to use open space

Reasons for move to the city

19% river erosion

13.5% uprooted

1.5% driven out

1.14% abandoned (elderly, children)

41%, came looking for work

The children not only live in tiny spaces, without basic amenities, but they also live in an environment of squalor and filth. Their dwellings are mostly constructed with any available scraps—cardboard, tin, plastic sheets. Open gutters, sewage water spewing close to the house, lack of open space to play or gather, rubbish dumped any and everywhere—a cause of offence to all the senses and breeding ground for disease-spreading insects and

> "I would like a nice house after I am married—somewhere clean and peaceful."
> — *Zohra*
>
> But what I dislike most is living in the *basti* is that there is no breathing space... only filth.
> — *Bilal*

rodents—are some of the immediate features the children have to cope with. Yet, their homes are clean and tidy. Perhaps therefore almost all of them expressed dismay and disgust with their surroundings.

> "I like the neighbourhood because people are always asking how I am. But the area around the house is very dirty. If we cannot find another house which is in cleaner locality, we will move back to the village."
>
> — Ahmed

Although some of the neighbours are caring enough, the children find their *bastis* filthy and crowded and have tried to make them better by different means. Bilal, for example, tried to grow vegetables but has had little success. Similarly Zohra is frustrated as all her attempts to improve her surroundings are foiled by others. She laments:

> What can be done? There are so many problems here. I don't like it when we make or organise something and others spoil it.

And Sarmin has the same complaint:

> Our slum is very dirty. People just throw things anywhere and everywhere. The thing I like about our neighbourhood is I can play around. What I don't like is you can't tell anyone to keep the place clean.

There appears to be no infrastructure, cooperation or community spirit which can make such changes possible. The children feel helpless and thwarted in their attempts to make their environment more liveable.

But Amina who works as domestic help in someone's house—and lives there—has a different experience:

> My Auntie's house, where I stay, has six rooms, fans, water, bathroom etc. I like the family I stay with. I like the things in the house. The furniture—I like it but I cannot sit on it. I just see it. There is a fridge and there is a TV also. We can watch the TV after we finish work. There are chairs and mirrors in the house. There is a gas stove in the house. The house has a garden with grass, flowers pots. I like the people in the house.

Many of the children, like Rahman, would undoubtedly feel a lot better about their existence if they had access to some amenities:

> I live in a house with a tin roof. There is a separate kitchen, there is electricity. There is a bathroom also. A tube-well is close by. I like the house because there is light, and it is an airy house.

Street children like Ali face problems on an entirely different scale. Their home is the streets of Dhaka, a city where public amenities are rare. To them even having a shared room, kitchen or toilet would be the ultimate luxury. They live a day at a time, at the mercy of others. Ali explains:

> I wake up and sometimes go to the centre for a bath, and also have breakfast there, other times I don't bother. I use the public toilet. Then if I have money in my pocket I have something to eat, else I manage without. When shops open, I go to the proprietors asking for work. I go from shop to shop but get nothing. No one gives work without some reference. Where can I get a reference from? Then I wander about a bit with my friends, talk to them, spend time with them in the park or whatever. Then it is night. Sometimes someone asks me to go home with them to give them a massage. Other times nothing. I just go off to sleep.

Violence and Crime

All parents try and shield their children from direct or indirect encounters with crime or violence. But in slums, where crime for many can be a

> "There are some *kala manush* (bad men) in the world. These people make bombs, they rob. I once saw a person being shot dead. There are some people who are addicted to drugs."
>
> — *Shahin*
>
> "I am afraid of *rangbaj*—if you just say a word to them they slap you. There are quite a few in our *basti*. They do business—they steal petrol from the petrol pumps and sell it elsewhere."
>
> — *Bilal*

career and violence a way of survival, the children can be protected only so much from knowing about such infringements or witnessing them. Beside the traffic on the streets of Dhaka, crime and violence are elements all these children fear and detest. Some of them have seen fights and scuffles in their *bastis* and around. One has seen someone being shot dead.

Traffic and Pollution

Chaos rules on the roads of Dhaka. From early morning until ten at night, the roads teem with buses, cars, taxis, auto rickshaws, cycle-

> Despite some recent changes in the kind of gas vehicles on the road can use, Dhaka remains one of the most polluted cities in the world. In many parts of the city there are open sewers, stagnating water and rubbish piled up on street corners. Around 6000 people die from pollution-caused illnesses in Dhaka per year.
>
> — *Sohel Islam, The Daily Star 20/7/03*

rickshaws, push carts and a variety of other transports. Rights to the road are appropriated by the size of the vehicles, and in this hierarchy the pedestrians have absolutely no rights. And as the majority of the

> High levels of noise is another irritant to the city dwellers, generated by car horns, general sounds on the streets, work on construction sites, road works (both of which have become a seamless feature of Dhaka city) and airplanes. In the day time noise levels reach as high as 90 to 100 decibels— well beyond the prescribed safety level (80 dcb).
>
> — *The Daily Star 21/7/03*

roads are without pavement, people share the roads with the trundling traffic and breathe in the toxic fumes it generates. The children have to face such traffic all on their own almost everyday. For many their walk to school takes between 20 to 40 minutes one way. Many parents are reluctant to send the young ones to school as they fear the traffic as much as the children do.

> One day I was going home from school. I was walking along the pavement and suddenly a speeding tempo hit me from the back. I was unconscious and hospitalised. I was very lucky that my medical cost was paid by the school.
>
> — *Ramon, age 10*

Living in poverty for these children means that not only do they have to live in congested, overcrowded, grimy environs and do without basic amenities, but they also get little respite from noise, pollution and tumult.

Ahmed

I have joined a samity. In that samity, I save Tk. 20 every day.

Ahmed is a student of the non-formal literacy classes at a school. He is bright and cheerful and happy at the thought of talking to me. He is dressed in clean clothes, and his hair is oiled and combed. He is thrilled that the interview will be recorded and delighted when I play the recording to him. Ahmed is also happy that I would be visiting his house and family.

My name is Ahmed. I am ten-years-old. I was born in a village in Kishoreganj. My family moved to Dhaka about three to four years ago. We moved because my father had to sell off everything to provide treatment for my grandfather who was very ill. We had our own house in the village. This house was also sold. My grandfather used to cough a lot. He died of this illness. My father had to borrow money t for the treatment, then he could not repay it.

Ahmed now lives in a small settlement very close to the school. There must be about 100 families in this area. This 7x7x8 room is home to three adults and five children. The room is built of thatch and bamboo. There is a fan and a light bulb in the room. A bed occupies most of the space in the room. There are shelves in the house where utensils are kept. There is a rack in a corner. For this space, the families pay Tk.500 per month. They feel more secure here as the landlord is supposed to take care of them.

Water is taken from a common tube-well. There are shared latrines in the colony. For about 200 people, there are two latrines and two bathrooms.

We used to live in a house in Gulshan. We had lived in that house for three-four years—ever since we moved from the village. Then the landlord told us to vacate it, and he broke down our house. He wanted to make his own house on that land. We now live in Battara. We have been living here for six months. I like the neighbourhood because people are always asking how I am. But the area around the house is very dirty. If we cannot find another house which is in a cleaner locality, we will move back to the village.

I have many relatives in the village. My nani (maternal grandmother) has a house there. My khala (mother's sister) and mama (mother's brother) also live there. I go to the village only to meet them. I like to play there. All people know us. They are always interested in us and ask how we are doing in the city.

I have an older brother who is fifteen-years-old. I also have two younger brothers. My sister is the youngest. She is only two-years-old. My father works in the school as the night guard. My mother works in a house. My parents

Ahmed's father is about 35-40 years of age. Ahmed's mother was away at work. When she goes to work, the father helps in looking after the children. He helps them clean up, gives them food and keeps an eye on them. On the day of the visit, the older brother and the grandmother were at home. The grandmother mentioned that she had another grandson, who had died. This child developed some kind of a skin disease and passed away.

cannot read and write. My elder brother also has never been to school. He works as a mistri (ironsmith) in a rod factory.

I work in the bazaar in Battara. I fetch water, cigarettes, paan (betel leaf), and tea for the clients of various shops. I earn taka 30-50 every day. I started work at the same time I started coming to school. I work in the evenings. I save taka 20 every day. The remaining I give to my mother. I have joined a samity (savings and loans group). In that samity, I save taka 20 every day. I have saved upto taka 1500. My father advised me to join the samity. I am saving the money for the new house. My employers treat me very well. I have no difficulty in coping with the work, my studies etc.

I like coming to the school. I like playing here. I like everything. I like the snacks. There is nothing difficult about the school. There was no money in our family; that is why I never went to school earlier. My parents tell me to study hard. They constantly encourage me. We learn how to write well, read well in the school. We are also taught about how to behave well with others. I like singing, reading and writing.

I help my mother in the house. I get water for her from the tube-well. I help in sweeping. If needed, sometimes I wash dishes also. My younger brother says I should do school work, and he offers to take care of the household chores with my mother. My elder brother does not help in the house.

I do not watch TV. A friend of mine has a walkman. He lets me listen to songs. I like listening to Hindi songs. I have seven friends in the neighbourhood. We play from 5 to 7 in the evenings. We play football and cricket. We bought the sets by contributing money. We take turns to keep the sets. My parents tell me to play well and not to fight. They tell me not to go too far from the house and the colony where I stay. All my friends work. They go to the mandir (temple) school. This school is for Hindus, but Muslims also go there. My friends are of different ages. We do not play with girls.

We celebrated Eid this year. On Eid day we sacrificed a goat. We distributed the meat.

One day my father got hurt in an accident. A truck ran over his leg. They had to operate upon him. He has a steel rod inserted in his leg now. It cost taka 2000. But the money that was given to him from the truck people was enough. I was very scared at that time. I thought my father was not going to get well. I cried a lot. My mother consoled me and told me that my father was going to be OK. I am scared of losing my parents. What will happen to my brothers, my sister and me then? Other than that I am not scared.

My parents tell me to beware of bad people. Children can get bad habits. They can get addicted to drugs (nasha korbe). They can also get into bad company. My neighbourhood people are nice; they always ask me how I am doing and if I would like to eat something. I am not scared of anything.

I want to be a driver, or a conductor. I think I would like to be a conductor. I will continue in the school when I finish this class. I will marry at the age of 30. I think before that is too young, and after that is too late. I will marry when I can keep my family happy. I will marry a girl who is 25 years. She should be educated. She should work in the house, and not outside. She should be able to read the Quran. I will marry the girl my parents select for me. She should be from a good family. I would like to have two children.

I do not know rich people. They do not have any problems. But I would not like to be rich myself.

Ahmed is a student of the recently established literacy class at a school for poor children. The literacy class is meant for children who have never been to school and are now past the formal school enrolment age. The literacy programme is a year-long programme with classes held four times a week. Neither of the parents is literate. But, the father understands that "without education there is no value." There is also a commitment to education despite the difficulties that might arise. As he says, "Even for a guard's job one needs to know how to read and write." He recognises the need for both girls and boys to be educated. However, if funds were a constraint, he would educate his sons.

Ahmed is always smiling and ready to explain things to me. He is ready to share his story with me. While Ahmed says he works after school, his father does not mention that his son is working.

Like other children his age, Ahmed too loves to play and listen to music. He and his friends contribute resources towards the funds needed for sports' equipment and also share in looking after it. This community feeling and social responsibility is rare amongst adults in the slum communities, especially when all energies are directed towards survival. Will Ahmed and his friends be able to sustain this feeling of working together when they grow up? Will they be able to develop this collaborative spirit into addressing larger issues that affect them all?

Bilal

Living in the city I have learnt that without money there is little freedom.

Bilal is a smart-looking, smart-talking teenager. He lives in the same *basti* as Mia, but in a much smaller room, which was constructed with whatever material was available. So some bits of the huts have plastic sheeting while other bits are cardboard. One side is a large piece of tin wall, and the other wall is from straw matting and some pieces of concrete. Father and son do their cooking just outside the hut. The mud stove is under a jute covering. Bilal has attempted to grow some vegetables on an empty plot opposite his home, but due to the soil—which is mainly sand and cement from the building work going on around the *basti*—and also lack of water, he has not had much success. Just beyond this plot is some more empty space, full of rubbish and stagnating water. Like all others interviewed, Bilal and his father have no possessions whatsoever besides the basics. The house has no electricity, and the water has to be fetched from 2-3 minutes distance.

My name is Bilal. I am thirteen-years-old. I live in Gulshan 2 by the lake. I have lived here for five years. Before this we lived in the village. We had to leave the village because we had no land or money. My father did not want to work as a labourer in the fields, and there is no other work in our desh (village). So we came to Dhaka. My father sells gas balloons here.

I have two sisters who are married in the desh. My mother lives in the village and I live here with my father. I like Dhaka—there is so much to see and do here. But in the village things are beautiful; there are less people. People are good, they are helpful. If some calamity befalls one, they come to one's aid. In Dhaka you don't get this. Here there is too much traffic and congestion, even walking anywhere is a problem.

My mother is in the village so here we have to cook ourselves and eat. My two sisters have studied up to Class VI, my mother up to Class II, but my father does not have any education. My father sends money to my mother in the village. She looks after the house there. She does not come to Dhaka. My mother does not like Dhaka. My nani (maternal grandmother) is there in the village. She lives near my mother. But my mother lives alone.

We live in one room here in Dhaka. We have no electricity or running water in the house. The toilet is by the lake—it is just a partition. We bathe in the lake. Many people use this toilet. People in the neighbourhood—many are good many are bad. Bad—like when I did something naughty, this person told my father and I got a beating for it. There are also good people like when I come home they ask me how I am, talk to me nicely. What I like about the neighbourhood is that I can play around. What I don't like is there are too many people. There is no bathroom, we have to bring water from elsewhere and there is much rubbish scattered about. Living in the city I have learnt that without money there is little freedom. One can't go around without money. Also, one has to be careful of the traffic.

I am poor because we have no money, I have to work while I am studying. We don't get enough to eat, can't go places. The rich have many things, big houses and trees. We poor have small houses, no fan or light, no electricity. The poor have many inconveniences.

I have been in school for four years. Without studies you can't do much. You can understand better through education and do things by yourself. If I go to a place and see a signboard I won't be able to read it unless I am literate. My father helps me with the homework but not always. We come back from selling balloons after 8-9 p.m., so sometimes I can't finish all of it at night, so I do it early morning. I can't always come to school in time because there are days we have to go and collect the balloons in the morning then I can't make it. I walk to school. It takes me about half an hour.

My father and I sell balloons in the evening. I start about 4 PM and work for four hours. On my return home I do homework and then we eat the leftovers. When I get home from school, unless my father has cooked, there is no food. I cook. I can make rice and vegetables. The money I make from selling the balloons I give it to my father. My father gives me pocket money—a little—every day. Sometimes I use it for taking the bus to the school, sometimes I buy biscuits, chewing gum and sometimes I save and buy toys. When I am selling the balloons, some people are OK some are not. Everyone is not the same in the world. Some people can be very fussy and will complain about a spot on the balloon.

At home I cook, make beds, sweep the floor, clean utensils. My father only does the cooking. I do miss my mother, I feel bad without her. I visit her in the village. When I go there people ask me a lot of questions about Dhaka. But I have difficulties. In the village people speak differently. In the village they speak the village language. In Dhaka they speak pure language so people tease me on how I speak when I am back in the village.

I do not have any fears at home even when I am on my own. Outside I worry about the traffic. I have no other worries. One thing I am afraid of is my father's beatings.

My father warns me not to mix with rangbaj (criminal) type of people or go to their homes. I am afraid of rangbaj—if you just say a word to them, they slap you. There are quite a few in our basti. They do business—they steal petrol from the petrol pump and sell it elsewhere.

I get tired working long hours. But I sit down when I get too tired. Sometimes I do not feel well. But generally I manage. I get a few hours free in the afternoon. Then I play with my friends. I play cricket, throw ball etc. I have three friends. One of them works with his father, and the other two are studying. My father tells me not to play with anyone who steals, or is a vagabond type. There is not much restriction from him except these, and that I should not go wandering.

There is a rich family near the basti. They have a three-storey house. There are four people in the family. Madam, Sir, one girl and one boy. The girl does not come into the basti. She calls us from her balcony and talks to us. The boy plays elsewhere. We are not allowed to enter their house. But when they see us, they behave well.

I am happiest when I can play. For Eid, I was selling balloons. At that time the sale goes up, so no holiday for me. I did not enjoy Eid. I just worked. After Eid I can enjoy, go out. The wedding of my sisters was in the village. There was much organisation and things to do. We played pranks on the bridegrooms. It was fun. In school we have fun activities in December, then there is Ekushey (21st February, the National Language Day) in February. The main thing that is wrong is that I don't like going to sell balloons. I know that if I don't do it, we won't get to eat. When I earn less, I worry. But I manage.

I have many wishes but they will not be fulfilled. I want to study more and do something. But it won't be possible, so I'll do what I can. I'll do business. At the age of 25 I would like to do some business other than selling balloons. I don't mind the balloon business but there is not much income in it. When I am older I want to go back to the village and live and work there because by the time I am older Dhaka will become more congested and dirty.

I would like to get married around 25-30 years age. I would like to marry someone who is below me, who is poorer than me. There is no good in marrying someone richer. I will have to give many things. I know someone richer will expect a car. We won't have one. They'll want clothes. I won't be able to give. Before getting married one should have a house, money, other things, then marry. I would like to have two children. It is easier to feed and clothe and manage with two. I have seen many families with 10-12 children, can't feed them properly, someone gets ill, some children have to work and they are still struggling. I will not demand dowry. My sisters' in-laws did not do so. Why should I? It is not a good practice. I don't know what my parents wish for me. They haven't said anything to me.

I like Rubel (a film star). He is a good fighter. I would like to learn to fight like him. I can't become a movie star just by wanting. I'll have to practice for it, and do it well.

Where I sell balloons I see a lot of rich people. Most of them behave well with me. Rich people don't look at poor people well. The rich have no problems. The poor have many problems: not enough food, no three meals, can't go where they wish, have to do hard work, living conditions are not comfortable, poor housing. I would like to be rich. I will study, will do business. Many people become rich by lottery. But I won't do bad things to be rich—I don't want that. If I don't become rich, so be it.

Sometimes I do not get three meals. I feel bad but manage. I get angry when I get home from school and there is no food. But what I dislike most is living in the basti. There is no breathing space—only filth.

My dream is to be become a bodo log (rich person). I have been working since the age of eight with my father. Sometimes I feel upset about having to work, but I know that there will be no food so I manage. I do not resent it but sometimes I get very tired. I would prefer to do something easier like shop work where I can at least sit.

Bilal's Father

I have been in Dhaka 20 years or so. I used to work in the factory but had to give it up as it was not regular work, so I went into the business of selling balloons. We live here without rent, but we know that we'll have to leave when we are asked to. We'll go wherever possible. We'll have to pay at the next place.

In the village the opportunities for work are less—not like Dhaka. We two (Bilal and I) work and support his mother and my sister. I feel bad living alone, but what choice does a poor person have? Without work we cannot eat. We manage with what we earn. I want Bilal to be educated. I want him to do well. I want him to study and do some service. As long as the school supports him to carry on his education, I will be glad for him to do so.

> The two things Bilal dislikes most about his life are selling balloons and living in the slum. He misses his mother. He left her behind in the village at the age of eight, and he has been selling balloons since then. Bilal wants to have work which is less taxing and which gives him a better income. But he is sharply aware that he will have even less to eat if he gives up this work. Despite everything that many families like Bilal's attempt to do (including migrating), they still do not get enough to eat. Both adults and children have to constantly worry about survival.

Migration and Poverty

Around 300,000 people migrate into Dhaka each year from the rural areas. Not having land or assets, becoming landless through floods or other natural calamities, being forced out of one's property by gangsters, losing all through debts, not finding gainful employment are not uncommon experiences in rural people's lives, forcing them to migrate to cities.

Migration from the village to the city is one event that has impacted on the majority of the children, contributing to this book, either directly or indirectly. Some families left as there was unrest in their village and some simply got pushed out of their legitimate right to home and property by crooks. In some cases whatever assets they had were eaten up by ill health or other causes. The children also talked about witnessing some families from minority communities being stripped of their homes and possessions by thugs. They watched families having to give up their land and having to move to other villages, and were concerned that these people had no assets left, like money or property, to build their lives elsewhere.

Loss of land and home through floods or other natural disasters and crop damage are other calamities driving people, who are already quite poor, into cities. Lack of job prospects in the rural areas further adds to the push factor. It is estimated that only 30 per cent of the population entering the labour force will be absorbed in the agriculture sector.[4] Break-up of large farm holdings into smaller ones means that land size is inadequate to support families. Despite both state and NGO supported programmes aimed at rural development, rural poverty continues to exist. While these programmes have boosted rural economy somewhat, they have not necessarily helped the poor. The control and influence by the elites over these organisations has also led to monopoly on gains. Absence of systems to prevent exploitation has led to the rich becoming richer and as a result (and despite the rural development programmes) the poor remain where they were, or are worse off.

Micro-credit programmes are limited in their scope. Aimed at reducing rural poverty by creating access to credit, without collateral, for the poor, these programmes have failed to reach the poorest of the poor. Participation in group meetings is considered essential to have

---

[4] See http://brandt.kurowski.net/projects/lsa/wiki/view.cgi?doc=819.

access to loans. Micro-credit programmes stay beyond the reach of those with no time to participate in lending organisations' programmes (like attending their meetings). Inadequate appreciation of market forces and increased local competition further affect both individuals as well as rural development.

Of the 12 children interviewed, 10 have come to Dhaka from rural areas. While it has not necessarily been a positive event in their lives, it has allowed them and their families to survive. Many, like Ahmed, don't much like living in the city but have little choice. In the villages their families neither have assets nor land nor work opportunities. He explains: "We moved because my father had to sell off everything to provide treatment for my grandfather who was very ill. We had our own house there, which was also sold. My grandfather used to cough a lot. He died of this illness. My father had to borrow money for the treatment. Then he could not repay it."

There is much that the children left behind when they moved to Dhaka. While Dhaka may provide them some material necessities and opportunities, it is the village that is more real to them, providing emotional sustenance of family and a caring community. Some of the children, like Bilal, are impressed by what Dhaka has to offer, and they already feel somewhat separated and alienated from the village people. Yet, they are not wholly comfortable with the people they associate with in Dhaka. Some experience alienation and deficit of social structures and networks. They sense a general lack of care and concern towards each other amongst the city people.

> "I like Dhaka. There is so much to see and do here. But in the village things are beautiful, there are less people. People are good, they are helpful. If some calamity befalls one, they come to one's aid. In Dhaka you don't get this."
>
> — *Bilal*

On top of the absence of rural community ties, life in Dhaka appears to provide only dangerous and difficult living. These children clearly feel that, despite its glamour and opportunities, Dhaka offers them little. They believe that they have exchanged space and greenery for dirt and squalor, peace and quiet for traffic and crowds. As Bilal elaborates, "Here there is too much traffic and congestion. Even walking anywhere is a problem. Places are very far and one needs to take a vehicle, but we can't [afford], so we have to walk."

Bilal and some others see their future in the village and want to go back as adults. Many migrants leave home with similar resolve but find it difficult to return to their roots for prospects don't seem to improve there. Unless the conditions for the rural communities are improved, economically and socially, Bilal or his children may end up back in Dhaka, living in inhuman conditions simply to survive.

While Dhaka offers opportunities for survival for thousands upon thousands of migrants pouring into the city each year, it plunges them into a life of chaos and social isolation. A recent report by the World Health Organisation (WHO) suggests that overcrowding in the city and rapid urbanisation is the cause for various kinds of psychological problems for the population. Around 10 per cent of Dhaka people experience hypersensitivity, depression, frustration, and other minor psychological anxieties which are now a serious cause of concern for health care providers.

But the city does offer physical survival. Even living on the streets, eating off the scrap heap or begging is a better option for some than starving in the village. As one boy puts it, "People either have to starve in their villages or move to the city and live in poverty here." And although limited, there are certainly opportunities in urban areas for work or self-employment, as well as possibilities for children to be educated. Ali, who has been living on the streets of Dhaka for the past six years and has often fallen foul of criminals, pimps, and police, says, "My mother wants me to stay in the village but there we can't eat. Here in Dhaka I can still get some work and manage."

Dhaka, it is better than the village. We have had problems—our last home was broken up but still we get to eat more regularly. In the village sometimes we only ate once in 2-3 days. Here if I go to people [where she used to work] and ask, people will give something or other, even clothes, because they have. In the village everyone is in the same situation. So how can they give what they don't have?

— *Mia's Grandmother*

And while Mia likes the open space and greenery of the village, he prefers to live his adult life in the city because his experience tells him that work in rural areas is scarce and subsistence a problem. This again raises the issues of both rural poverty and lack of employment opportunities. Survival in village communities for most seems to hinge on ownership of land or property.

Most of the children see life in Dhaka fraught with risks. Yet they know that they gain in different ways. Urbanisation seems, in their case, to lead to the development of a more positive self-image. The way they speak, walk and conduct themselves changes to some extent and causes a

> People treat me very well there because I go after a long time. I need pants, shirts before I go back to the village.
>
> — *Rahman*

separation between them and their relatives and friends living in the village—a divide of status, language and mannerism. Some also feel that rural areas offer nothing other than agricultural work and therefore, despite their affection for their village, would prefer to continue living in the city.

> When I go there [the village] people ask me a lot of questions about Dhaka. But I have difficulties. In the village people speak differently. In the village they speak the village language. In Dhaka they speak pure language so people tease me on how I speak when I am there.
>
> — *Bilal*

But another peril of living in the city, which all the children interviewed have experienced, is having to move house. In affluent communities moving house, although considered as a stressful event, generally means moving into something better. For most slum dwellers when their patched-together homes are demolished—to build yet another shopping plaza or apartment block—they just have to move to another area. All the children in our study have had to move at least once. Most of the slums in a city like Dhaka, which is constantly expanding, spring up next to building sites or a near enough open space. The shantytown itself expands till such time that the landowner re-claims it for building.

> Near the Osmani Udyan, Bangladesh Railway bulldozed around 1200 shanties, leaving more than 5000 people homeless.
>
> — *The Daily Star* 18/2/03

At the age of nine Mohammad watched his home being destroyed and the family having to move to another slum. They had already moved once from the village when Mohammad was two, seeking a livelihood. He in fact is amongst the lucky ones to have been uprooted only twice. There are some children who have, in their short life, moved home three or four times and expect to do so again. Mohammad narrates, "They broke our place down and told us to leave with our stuff. The landlord did that, he built a garage there." Mia still feels grieved about moving, "The landlord there asked us to leave. He said he'd build a house there so we had to leave. He has made a six-storey apartment block there."

> Bangladesh Railway knocked down an illegal slum on its land at Tejgaon in the city. It also forced the squatters to board the wagon with their belongings for an unknown destination.
>
> — *The Daily Star* 12/3/03

Another consequence of migration or moving house is loss of democratic rights. Sarmin's mother says that she does not vote as she is registered to vote in the area they previously lived in (ten years ago). This is not a unique situation. A large number of the population shifting from rural to urban or from place to place, for various reasons, end up in a position where they are required to go back to their original address to vote in local and national elections or not vote at all. It is the poor migrants who are more vulnerable as not only do they move more often but also they have little spare money to travel back simply to exercise their democratic right to vote. People living in poverty therefore end up having even less say in the system and get pushed more to the fringes of society.

Zohra

There was no work in the village. We could not manage. My father got work in Dhaka. Now it is a bit better.

Zohra is a slim, tall girl, mostly with a serious look on her face. I meet her at the school and we take a rickshaw to her home—a 20-minute ride. Normally, from her home Zohra has to walk for 40 to 50 minutes to get to school. A mud path from her house meets the main road. This is a very busy road—from the airport into the town centre. Trucks, buses, cars, auto-rickshaws all speed up and down this main artery. Her house, made with straw matting and polythene, is on stilts over a pond. A bridge connects the house to the bank. It is like the homes of the majority living in the slums, one small room, almost 8x8 feet, with bare essentials for the family of four adults and five children. Cooking is done at the mosque and eaten either in the house or outside. The house and the area are kept clean. But during the rainy season, the outside gets flooded and slushy. In fact Zohra's hut is the only one left in that location. There are no houses facing them but very near there is a semi-concrete block of homes where the slightly better off reside in their one room abode. Since her father lost his job, Zohra's family lives with his uncle, aunt and their child.

My name is Zohra and I am twelve-years-old. I have lived in Dhaka for four to five years. I was born in my village. My father has been in Dhaka for 12 years. There was no work in the village. We could not manage. My father got work in Dhaka. Now it is a bit better. There we have no land, we didn't have enough to eat. Nothing. How could we manage? So we came to Dhaka. I liked it in the village. We could go around. I still go to the village, may be once a year. I like it there. My grandparents are there. My grandfather works on someone's field. People treat me nice. They invite me to their home, ask me to eat things. I like roaming around in the village, seeing things, I like being with my grandparents. I like the people of my village, they are very nice.

In Dhaka I don't like the traffic and the pollution. I don't like the behaviour of the people in Dhaka. What I like here is living with my parents, going to different places, studying. I have four brothers and one sister in my family and my parents. My father sells vegetables in the market. My mother works in someone's home. It's a three-storey brick house. My brothers are studying, and I and my younger sister are in this school. My parents have no education. My parents are working very hard to educate my brothers so they can become manush [something].

We are poor. How can we be rich? We have nothing. We have no money. How can we have a two-three storey house? We have one room. We do our cooking just outside, on a mud stove. In my house we have one bed and one chair. We have water out side—it is about one minute away. We have our bath there. When we go to fetch water, we have a bath. It is an open area with a polythene partition. We bathe with our clothes on. We wash our clothes there one at a time. It is hard to do them all together. We have no electricity. We have lamps. The toilet is a structure with bamboo matting on three sides. Three to four families use it. All of us have these houses on rent. What can be done? There are so many difficulties here. For a broken down place we have to pay 400-500 rent. We don't have money for a brick house.

I like playing with friends here.... I like it very much. But I don't like the dirt and squalor. I don't like when we make or organise something and others spoil it.

I have been in school for four years. I wanted to go to school. It was in my heart that my parents are not educated, if I know how to read and write.... My parents also talked to me. I know some boys and girls who go to other schools. For us with less money this school is good. If I am educated then I can get a good job and look after my parents. Here I have learnt good manners. I have learnt how to behave well with others, reading and writing. I like games and sitting under the tree. I do the homework with the kuppi light. It is very difficult. My parents and brother help and encourage me. They say, "I'll sit with you, you write, I watch the lamp does not go out, write well so you will get praise at school." I walk to school. Sometimes if I am given money I come by bus. It costs me one taka by bus. Walking takes 40 minutes.

At home I wash clothes, I tidy up, sweep and mop the house. I do all the housework as I am the older sister. Others don't do it I have to do it. I can't be jealous of others. My sister helps a little when I am cooking. My mother leaves in the morning and comes back at night—8 o'clock.

When my brother gets back from school he does some tasks—tidying, brings water, helps me with the cooking. We all fetch water according to who is free. My father goes out very early—does not get time even to eat. Then he comes back at 1 o' clock.

Once a week my parents give me two taka. I save the two taka. My mother and father don't know. I don't buy anything.

I have to do all the housework, there is no choice. Later on I do my homework. When I get a little free time, I play. There are some girls and boys whom I like, I play with them hide and seek, catch-me, hopscotch. Sometimes we just run around. When I have difficulties with homework I ask for help.

Sometimes I get upset that we don't have much in our house—just one cot and a broken chair. If guests come where can I ask them to sit?

Around us there are people with more money than us and also with less. The ones richer than us have TV. Sometimes I would like to go and watch TV there but they don't let me. When their children come to play, sometimes I don't play with them as I feel hurt.

I am not much afraid about the future. But if my mother is ill I get very afraid. I worry if she dies what will I do? If my father is not there and it is night-time and no one can come to help, what will I do?

We couldn't do much for Eid. What can we do? We did not even have shemai. We had no money so we all just stayed at home.

My father had money problem one time. I gave him 100-200 taka. I was much pained we did not have anything to eat. Whatever money I had saved, I took that out and gave it to him. I was upset. Once we were invited to some rich people's party near us. I was really happy. But what could we do? We had no decent clothes. We would not have been able to give any present. We could not go. I was very upset.

It will not be possible for me to continue with my studies. I will have to work in someone's house. I would like to study further and do better. After my studies I would like to be a doctor. But for someone like me it is not possible to find so much money to become a doctor. I do not wish to marry now or when I am 25. But marriage will happen. As I grow older, if I am not married, people will say, "The girl is so big and they are not getting her married." But how can one get married without meeting the demands [of dowry]? How can we give what is desired? I don't want to get married till I am at least 30. I will have one girl and one boy. If I have too many what will we eat? A small family is good. I would like a good husband—one who does not ask for dowry, doesn't take this or that, does not behave badly with me, doesn't smoke and drink. I want him to be economically like me—not too rich. What will I do with someone rich? Rich people are good but I want someone good. Good behaviour is more important.

Although my parents want me to study, they don't have the money to make me a doctor. They will ask me to work in someone's house. I want to be like Sabina [a popular singer]. She is a very good singer and I want to learn to be as good as her. I would like a nice house after I am married—somewhere clean and peaceful. Yes I want to be rich, but wanting something does not mean one gets it. People become rich through education, through big jobs. No one will give me a big job. If one tries one can be anything, but I haven't the money to bribe for a good job.

We eat two meals a day. Sometimes my mother is given food where she works and brings it home. Sometimes we do not have sufficient food to eat and go partially hungry.

When people behave with me nicely, when they play with me OK, when all is well with my parents I am happy.

I get most angry if someone nags me.

My dream is to live in a nice house, have enough to eat, have clothes.

Zohra's Father

In my life I have put up with much hardship. Since I came to Dhaka—I was seventeen then—20 years ago I have struggled for a livelihood. I have pulled rickshaws, carried loads on my head—I ended up with a bald patch with that—made bricks, pushed carts, did odd jobs and finally I got a job as a guard in the bank. From there I moved to the manager's home as a guard. I was there for three years but last year the family left and I have not been able to find another job. This last year I have done nothing but look for a job—but no luck. I have certificates but they have not been helpful either.

My uncle is unwell. Two years ago he had a stroke and is paralysed on the left side. I in fact came to Dhaka as a youngster to my uncle. My parents and other family members are in the village. My parents had no land or money so I came here, but here I can't make enough to help them in any way. My uncle used to grow crops in this place, there used to be a river running through here. There were no houses or shops. The land belongs to someone else. He has allowed my uncle to live here free of charge for the last 20 years. But you can see how it is developing. So we think our days are numbered here. I am not educated, but I want my children to be so they can get some job, have a better life than me. With all the hard work I have not managed to provide two meals a day for my family. So I feel that without education there is no future. In Bangladesh the majority of people are in this situation. With education they will learn manners and be good people. I have struggled very hard. It has been a tough life. My main wish is to educate my children, and I am grateful for the free school.

Zohra's father and other members of the family are most welcoming. There is an acceptance (but not resignation) of their meagre living conditions and what life has accorded them. Zohra, very sensitive to her family's situation, is only too well aware that both her parents work hard to make sure her brothers are educated. She does not expect her parents to educate her as well. In fact Zohra's mother is away working for the best part of the day even though her health is suffering. Her father's health is none too good either. Zohra is therefore prepared to stop studies and take on paid work. She seems to be conscious of the problems poverty has caused them and fears for them—especially her mother. She would rather not marry and look after her family and is certainly prepared to give up her hopes and dreams for the good of her family. One can't but feel her sense of resignation to fate and the sadness she carries within her.

Gender Roles, Responsibilities and Equality

There are a large number of organisations (rural and urban) in Bangladesh working with and for the welfare and rights of women. There are also some very strong women spearheading the struggle for equal rights and an equal place for women in society. And although women in this country can be found working in almost every sphere of life, but in general, like in many other parts of the world, economically they remain dependent upon and deferential to the male members of the family or at the workplace. Their status and place in society is quite defined and very few cross the line—even some of the educated and economically liberated ones more or less conform to the expected norms.

While gender roles and responsibilities and children's reactions to these were explored in general in the focus group discussions and the individual interviews, two separate focus groups were also conducted, one for girls and another for boys, in which the topic of discussion was solely around the subject of the treatment of girls within the family and outside the home by society in general. Parents were also asked for their thoughts on the difference in the treatment of sons and daughters.

The children, both boys and girls, are familiar with the prevailing situation for girls and women in society. Discrimination sets in early and so does the realisation. The majority of the children, even if they have witnessed instances to the contrary, accept the restrictions, spoken and unspoken ones, put upon girls and women. Many of the girls resent this but obey the rules all the same, for sometimes the consequences for defiance can be severe.

The concept of "shame" and "modesty" is a heavy cloud which the girls have to constantly live under. Anything that a girl does that is against the norm brings shame not only to her but her whole family, which in turn determines the family's relationships within the community (as well as that of the individuals in the family). This concept is imbibed and internalised by girls (and boys) from a very early age.

All who participated in the discussion (twelve girls between the ages of 10 and 14 and eight boys also in the 10 to 14 age group) were in agreement that rules set by society are different for girls and boys, that there are more restrictions put on girls. But, they contended, the same did not apply to girls from rich families. The rich, it was strongly felt, live by their own rules.

Their Views

Both groups concur that all children are expected to be good, but the definition of "good" is clearly different for girls than it is for boys. A good girl behaves well, she studies well and is good with everyone; she does not fight; she maintains a concept of decorum and "shame;" she does not roam around and does not do anything without her parents' permission. While these attributes of goodness apply to boys also (from rich or poor families), there is one major exception. Boys, even if they roam around or stay out late in the evening remain "good," while girls for doing the same are labelled, "bad."

Both girls and boys consider boys as being physically stronger and therefore more able to do physical labour like pulling rickshaws and doing building work. Girls are considered better at cooking and shopping for food. Both agree that boys do undertake these tasks but are not very good at them.

A few girls have been seen driving rickshaws, riding bikes, selling ice cream on pedal-vans and hawking peanuts. The boys believe that these girls have little choice. Poverty simply forces them to take on these jobs. "They do it for the stomach." Some girls believe that "Girls remain indoors because of the sense of shame or shyness girls feel and so cannot do work outside the house and end up doing house work." Thus in poor families "good" girls do house work and "good" boys bring in earnings for their parents.

The girls argue that if they ride bikes or pull rickshaws, people will make derogatory comments. They suggest that in any case their parents will find such activities unacceptable. Some rich girls have been seen riding bikes and motorbikes but even they dress up in boys' clothes to disguise themselves. One girl very poignantly says, "I also wish to do the same but I know my parents will not allow. They will say you are a big girl now. You cannot do these things. But no one can say anything to rich people."

The girls also indicate that when they are young there is little difference between boys and girls, and both do almost the same things—play, education and responsibilities are similar. However, once they are a little older, things change. Girls can't go out to play while boys can. Girls are given less and boys more. Their education is blocked in preference for boys being educated. Girls are advised that studies are not important for them and told that the boys will have to work so they will have to be educated. And duties also get divided on gender lines. But once again the perception is that the rich girls do not experience the same treatment.

Rich girls can get good education, can become doctors if they like. Poor girls, on the other hand, as soon as they are grown up are married off. "Then she has to look after her husband, her in-laws. She cannot play, can't loiter around."

The girls suggest that in poor homes girls get less to eat, that parents tell them, for example, not to eat too much of tomato (expensive item at the time of discussion) and urge boys to eat more and girls are asked to do more work and eat less. The girls argue that this is the rule of society. "Our parents tell us, 'You should not grow too big. What will you do by being so big? Let the boys eat." The boys, however, believe that parents behave the same with their children. They all get the same food; it gets divided equally and all eat together.

The girls feel bad that "The girls and boys do same work but get treated different." They point out that poor girls, even when they have a job outside the home, still have to do much work round the house. "But rich girls do not have to work at home. They only work in the office as they have servants in the house. They can study. They also go out with friends and play with them and go for walks."

The girls suggest that "When boys grow up they have to go out to work but they still have three to four hours free time for leisure. They can play, they can roam around. But girls even if they are working, like in a garment factory, or studying, when they get home they have to work." Many girls argued that "It is better for girls not to work outside because when they come home after a day's work they still have to do house work anyway." But others believe that "Work outside home means girls can earn money that way if the husband is not good, and he refuses to work so what can one do—no food without work—so the wife will have to work."

The girls deplore this discrimination. "This is not right. Boys get away with so much. If they are asked to do something, they can say no and get away. What can the girl do? She just has to obey."

Shahin

I like Dhaka better. There is a school here. We can learn to read and write. People talk well here.

Shahin and I meet at the school after his class is over. This was his first year at the school. His clothes are well worn and his hair is brownish in colour—probably a result of malnutrition. Shahin is uncomfortable and anxious about the meeting. He speaks rapidly and very softly. He leans forward to talk to me. He answers in short sentences. In the second meeting he is more relaxed and willing to share information.

My name is Shahin. I am nine-years-old. I work at Wonderland—in a food shop.

My family is originally from Kishoreganj. I do not know when my family moved away from the village. There are eight of us at home—my grandmother, sisters, brother, mother, father, uncle and aunt. My father has a van gadi and mother stays at home. Neither my mother nor my father has been to school. My uncle is a labourer. I have two sisters and a brother. My sisters are younger than me; one is six and the youngest is two and a half-years-old. My grandmother takes care of my little sister.

My brother, who is 12-years-old, has gone to the village to look for work. He has gone to Kishoreganj. He used to be in the literacy class. I had another sister who died when she was three. She had diarrhoea in the morning and she died by the evening. She was number four in the family.

Our home is made of cardboard. There are two rooms. There is a tube-well and a hurricane lamp. There is a papaya tree. I like my house.

I like the school. I like reading and singing. My favourite song is "Dere bhalo, man chahe na." I do not like to play games. Once I got hurt from a soda bottle and cut my hand. I needed an injection afterwards. I like the Ferris wheel at Wonderland. Because I work there, I get free rides at Wonderland.

I work from nine in the morning to nine in the evening. I come to school at 11 AM . My work is to clean and serve for which I get taka 200 (approximately USD 3) per month. I give the money to the family to run the house. I keep taka 20 for myself from which I eat, and sometimes have a 7 UP also. I come to school in a tempo which costs taka 4. My employer treats me well. He gives me food, rice, vegetables. I don't eat mangoes as mangoes can give worms.

I study at home after 9 PM with a lamp. My parents help by encouraging me. I also have free time, from 12 to 2 PM when I study. I help in the house by fetching water. I like to play with my little sister. Sometimes I take her for a walk.

There are some kala manush (bad men) in the world. These people make bombs, they rob. I once saw a person being shot dead. There are some people who are addicted to drugs.

I like the toy train at Wonderland, and also the food there. We celebrated my little sister's birthday. My baba [father] bought a cake, a plain cake. There were about ten people at the party and we had food together.

I went to the village recently with my mother. My uncle, my mother's brother, was unwell. My uncle had jaundice and could not eat anything. We got a letter from the village informing us that he was unwell and that we should go and see him. My uncle has no land. He has a few goats. I was in the village for a month. I played with my cousins while I was there. While I was there, I could not see my brother who lives with my mother's sister in another village.

Although I had fun in the village, I like Dhaka better. There is a school here, we can learn to read and write. People talk well here. I would like to study further once this literacy class is over. I would like to study—may be at the model school. I would like to go to the model school because everyone goes there. The model school is till Class V. I might work also. I would like to work in a house.

When I am 18-25-years-old, I would like to be a durban [guard] because the durban opens the doors and lets the cars in. When I am my parent's age then I would like to drive a car—my own car.

I would like to marry when I am 24-25-years-old. I would like to marry a bhalo girl. She should be able to read and write. She should stay at home. I would like to live with my parents at my home. I would like to have 2-3 children, both girls and boys. I will get them to study.

I admire Momota—a girl in my neighbourhood. She works at someone's home.

I think we are poor; we do not have TV. There is no safe in our house. I have been to rich people's houses. They have lots of things. They talk well. Some rich people want well of the poor. They think well of the poor. Some shopkeepers do not treat me well because I am poor. The rich do not have any problems.

I would not want to be rich. The police come and catch rich people. Then they have to pay money to be released. The police take away rich/good people. They leave the poor people. This happens where I live.

I dream that the future will be good. "Bhalo he hobe."

Shahin lives in a slum on the banks of the lake in Gulshan. His family of six adults and three children share the space. The house is on solid ground. The house is built on uneven land, flush against the boundary wall of a multi-storeyed building. There are three parts to the house: a small verandah where the visitors are entertained; a bedroom and a courtyard at the back. There are cots and almirahs in the house along with trunks. There are also a few hens and their chicks. Cooking is done in the courtyard or outside on the dirt road. Drinking water is obtained from nearby buildings. Bathing and washing of clothes is done in the lake. *Kaccha* (unpaved) latrines are around the corner. The house is rent-free.

Shahin's Family

At the time of the visit, only Shahin's mother and his two sisters were at home. The mother and Shahin had recently returned from the village. They had gone to visit Shahin's uncle (mother's brother who was unwell). Shahin's parents are not educated. His mother does not work outside the house. Shahin's mother was reticent and less willing to talk about her children—maybe because this was her first meeting with the author. She might also have been inhibited by the presence of more articulate and confident neighbours who had no hesitation in voicing their opinions. Shahin's mother was quite happy with her son's ability to work and to study. She indicated that she would like to have her girls go to school as well. She was concerned with how children tended to listen less and less to their parents these days, especially as they grew older.

According to her, there were few places the poor could go to for health care. The doctor who came every Tuesday and Friday at the mosque gave free consultation. One still needed to buy the medicines. In the event of need on other days, there was no recourse but to go to the private doctor who charged taka 300 per visit. Immunisations were available during the camps held in the parks. Her children had been immunised at these camps.

If appearance could be used to determine the degree of poverty, then Shahin would be ranked as one of the poorer ones. His clothes are shabby and he has an unkempt look about him. He speaks very fast and in a low voice, almost as if he does not want anyone to overhear what he is saying. It took much longer to get him to talk about himself than it did with the other

Continued

Continued

children. Shahin's family story shows how the move from village to Dhaka and back happens when things do not work out well. His brother, who was also in the literacy class, had to go back to the village as there was no work for him in the city. It is also a story of how poverty keeps families apart. Shahin and his mother could not visit the brother who lived in another village in the same district as his uncle. Shahin has witnessed violence and seems to live in proximity to violence. His fear of playing or eating mangoes seems to have gone beyond their rational causes.

Mohammad

In truth I would like to get a job but that is not going to be easy as for jobs first you need money to bribe.

Mohammad is ten years of age but physically looks smaller. He always seems to have a very serious look on his face. His family moved from the village to Dhaka around ten years ago as in the village they had no land or any other asset to support a livelihood. But life in Dhaka has not been easy either. Starting from scratch—doing any job that came along—Mohammad's father has risen to guard duty in a supermarket. In fact, four family members work full time. Yet, often two meals a day are not possible for the family.

My name is Mohammad and I am ten-years-old. I live in Shahjadpur. I have lived in this house for about four months. Before this I used to live behind Azad Mosque. They broke our place down and told us to leave with our stuff. The landlord did that; he built a garage there. We lived there for eight years; before that we were in the village. My father came for work to Dhaka. In the village he had no work and we don't have any land there. We have been in Dhaka ten years. We go to the village very rarely. We have no family there. My grandparents are dead.

My house is on stilts on the lake. It is made with bamboo. We are eight in my family: my sister-in-law, my elder brother, two other brothers, myself, my parents and my brother's five-month-old baby.

My mother works in someone's house and my father works in a shop. My parents are not educated. My brothers are—one has studied up to Class VIII, the other up to VII. One is studying in Class VI, and I am here in Class III. My brother works at the same shop as my father. My sister-in-law has studied up to Class VIII. She did not work before marriage.

We are a poor family. We have no land in the village. In Dhaka we work, and whatever we make is not sufficient. With that we cannot buy things and clothes. Mostly we eat three times a day, but sometimes only twice. We don't have TV. I have not been to the cinema.

We live in a basti. Our house is just one room. We all live in one room. We eat in that room and also sleep there. The bathroom is outside and is used by other neighbours as well. The toilet is by the bathroom. We get water from the tap which is by the bathroom. We have electricity. We have a fan and light. I like my basti. It is well organised. But I don't like the slush and wet parts. People are nice. They don't do anything bad.

I am in Class III at school. I could not attend school before, as it requires money. Other schools charge money. I like games and studies and poems and stories. My parents wanted me to come to school but we did not have the means. I did not know then that getting education has such benefits. You can get jobs—big jobs—one can be a doctor, a policeman. I walk to school. It takes me half an hour. My family helps me with the homework. They encourage me to study well.

I help my sister-in-law in the house. I bring her water to wash the rice, vegetables, clean the stove. I play with the baby, carry him around and sometimes sing. My bhabi [sister-in-law] feeds him. My brother also helps in fetching water; he holds the baby.

My parents give me pocket money, but not everyday. Once every two to three days. I buy some things I want—biscuits, sweets....

I wander around in my free time, alone. My friends go to school in the afternoon. On Friday and Saturday, I play football. I have a friend, Arif, in the basti. My parents do not stop me from playing with anyone I want. I do have fears. Many new people come into the basti and I fear them. They can rob us. Our neighbours who live opposite our house got robbed. They took everything.

Playing cricket makes me happiest. Eid also makes me happy. For Eid I went out, my parents got me new clothes. Everyday we don't take big meals. Sometimes we have rice and fish and some days, vegetable. For Eid we had shemai [vermicelli], polao [fried rice dish] and chicken.

I was eight when my brother got married. I remember his weeding—it was great, I really enjoyed it. I played tricks. At night we blackened my bhabi's [sister-in-law] sister's face while she was asleep. We had singing and dancing.

We had a bad event in our family. My brother got kidney stones. He needed 10,000 taka for treatment. We had to go to Tangail for it. I was seven-years-old then. I was really fearful. What if my brother does not get better, he will die.

After finishing school here, I will look for a job. If I don't get a job, I'll try and study to be a doctor. But that costs a lot of money and so if that is not possible I'll do fish business. It will cost less than studying to be a doctor. In truth I would like to get a job, but that is not going to be easy as for jobs first you need money to bribe. So I want to do fish business because I can go to the river, catch fish and sell them.

I would like to marry when I am grown up, when I am 20. I would like the girl to be beautiful and educated and to be able to read Arabic. It is the language of our religion. I know Arabic. I want her to be from a small family and not very rich. She can adjust better in a poor environment if she is from same background. I don't like rich people....

I would like to have two-three children. A small family is good. One can manage with a small family not with big. I don't think it is good to marry early. I'll marry when I am 20. My parents have told me not to marry early. I don't know why. I would like to live in my village after I am married. I like going there. There one doesn't have to be fearful, one can walk around peacefully. In Dhaka people behave badly (dushtami), they fight, I have seen it near my basti.

I wanted to be rich but not any more. Can't get big job, can't be a big doctor. Doing fish business all can't become big people. If one has luck one can become big. My parents want me to be a big businessman, or a doctor. I respect my parents most. I also love my nephew. If someone swears at me I get very upset. And if someone hassles me, it makes me angry. My dream is to be a doctor.

Mohammad lives in a room in a *basti*, with his two brothers and parents. His married brother has a room of the same size three doors away for himself, his wife and their five-month-old baby. But the family meals are cooked and eaten together. Their cooking facilities are down the lane and round the corner in a communal kitchen shared by 50 families. They are very lucky to have piped gas in the kitchen and electricity in the *basti*. As Mohammad explains, "The *basti* is well organised and facilities are good" and therefore he likes living there. Also he says that "The *basti* people are nice and don't do anything bad." The *basti* stretches about half a mile on the east bank of the Gulshan Lake and spreads a quarter of a mile in. The *basti* is built mostly on stilts—including many of the walkways—and has 500 families living in similar one-room homes. There are rows upon rows of rooms, all tightly packed, with absolutely no outdoor space to spare, just walkways between rows. There is no greenery or space for children to run about or people to gather. The little room that Mohammad lives in is basically an 8'x 8' hut with tin walls, tin roof and wooden floor. Three of the walls are shared and through the wooden slats on the floor one can see the lake water and all the muck floating on it. There was stench in the air, but it was not as bad as it would be in summer. On the day of the visit (late March) there was a freak storm, and what with the radio on one side and a baby crying on the other and the rain drumming on the tin roof, one could not hear oneself talking. With each gust of wind this structure on stilts shook. One can imagine what it would be like during the monsoon with incessant rain and wind every day of the week for three months or so. In fact the family told me that in the rainy season the

Continued

Continued from Mohammad

lake rises, flooding all the paths and thereby cutting them off from all amenities such as schools, doctors, market etc. During this period the road connecting them to such facilities is only reachable via boat.

Mohammad is somewhat reluctant to admit that he helps in the house. In fact, almost all boys we spoke to—even when there are girls in the family—do some domestic chores. Most were happy enough to admit to this.

Mohammad's earnest desire is to be a doctor, perhaps because he associates the profession with status and wealthy people (*bhadralog*). But he is ambiguous about being rich, and is fully aware of his family's financial circumstances. They can neither afford to send him for studies beyond primary level, nor do they have the means to bribe anyone for a decent job for Mohammad. He is wise enough to have plan B, i.e. go into the fish business.

Corruption

If one tries, one can be anything but I haven't the money to bribe for a good job.

— *Zohra*

Talk to anyone in Bangladesh and they will tell you how corruption has increased over the years, and how even ordinary civil servants now can manage to live in grand houses and send their children to private schools, something way beyond their meagre salaries. This corruption is all-pervasive from top to bottom, and it is not always money changing hands. Teachers in government schools, it is said, sign in the morning, walk into class, take the attendance, appoint a child to manage the class, and disappear for the day to do another job.

Yet it would be only fair to emphasise that the problem of corruption is not exclusive to Bangladesh. It is an affliction of the rich as well as the poor countries. However, while in rich countries serious corruption is mainly confined to the higher echelons of the system, in poor countries like Bangladesh it is all-encompassing—impacting on everyone's lives. Thus one thing in favour of Bangladeshi corruption is that it can be said to be, as we term it, "democracy of corruption" where all are allowed to partake in the system of bribery, fraud and vice, not just some privileged few at the top. In rich countries corruption both in the private and public sectors can be of such magnitude that an individual's take could easily match the GDP of a poor country. The other distinction between corruption in rich and poor countries is that while in the wealthier parts of the world the general public does not experience the impact of dishonesty and fraud directly—except through taxes perhaps—in less well-off countries everyone, particularly the poor, are hit hard by such practices in every-which way on a daily basis.

Corruption for people living in poverty sadly acts as a double jeopardy. It is not only a factor contributing to poverty but also often making it worse. At one level the full value of any project and programme intended for the poor is not always realised by the poor and second, to gain a foot-hold on any rung of improvement or even to get a simple service or fair treatment, the poor do not have the money or other resources to bribe, influence or buy off officials or their minions (a prerequisite in a corrupt society). The President of the International Development Association and the International Finance Corporation points out that the poor in fact face a disproportionate amount of problems due to corruption in

"In the name of poverty reduction, the government has finalised a Tk 13.5 crore technical assistance project, stuffing it with air conditioners, cars and foreign tours."

The Public Expenditure Review Commission (PERC) said, "This project is an unwarranted waste of government resources and has manifested a prime example of being irrelevant to the real needs."

— *Rejaul Karim Byron, The Daily Star, 23/8/03*

society. "They are forced to go without access to power and water because they cannot afford the illicit payments necessary to secure connections. They receive lower quality health and education services since they cannot pay bribes to those who control access to medical services, education materials and credit."[5] Of course sometimes it also works the other way round when votes of the poor are bought through patronage or hard cash.

A study conducted by the Bangladesh Rural Advancement Committee (BRAC), shows how a small number of people from a select band in rural Bangladesh built a system of contacts and associations, thereby appropriating control over scant public and private resources and in turn controlling the disbursement of these resources.[6] The research suggests that due to the entrenched corrupt practices of the powerful elite, many of whom are members of political parties, the benefits simply do not reach the ones who actually need them.

The same study also shows that the powerful, through their privileged position and relations with the government (local and central) and through threats of

My grandparents had land in the village but there was *gondogol* [trouble] and they had to leave and come to Dhaka.

— *Mia*

violence (often actual), are able to usurp land and other resources belonging to the poor. Many such dispossessed ultimately end up in cities for survival.

The services the poor receive, if at all, from professionals such as doctors, police, teachers etc. are largely questionable. The same BRAC study, for example, also suggests that doctors often give their poor patients low-cost medicine as opposed to what they provide for the well off and yet bill the government at the higher rate.[7] In urban slum

---

5   Wolfenshon, 2000.

6   BRAC, 1986.

7   ibid.

Just a week after a World Bank paper reported that 74 per cent of the doctors do not attend duty, in a surprise visit to the National Institute of Cardiovascular Diseases, the Director General of Health Directorate found 24 of 28 on-duty doctors to be absent.

— The Daily Star Report, 2/10/03

communities the poor have to pay high fees to private doctors, for often there are no government health facilities nearby and where there are the doctors are mostly unavailable. Also patients are expected to give *baksheesh* (donation/bribe/tip) to the "gatekeepers" of such facilities before receiving any service.

Those children who do end up in government schools (as they can't afford private schooling and may not be lucky enough to have an NGO school in the vicinity) get very little (if any at all) education, thus leaving them weaker or incapable of competing for jobs and making the most of other opportunities. It is a known fact that children in Bangladesh have to have tuition to pass exams, and many school teachers supplement their income by giving private coaching. Thus it is in their interest not to teach appropriately during the school hours. But the poor who can scarcely afford two meals a day can hardly be expected to find tuition fees.

Needless to say, the police and other related services are also on the take. Shahidul Alam tells the story of 14-years-old Rimon, a rickshaw puller, who was wrongfully arrested, with evidence planted on him. He was kept in jail for two years without trial. His mother, Fatema, who worked seven days a week for meagre wages as a domestic servant, borrowed 20 times her salary to raise money for her son's trial. Alam writes, "The process of trying to bribe judges, paying high fees to lawyers and regularly paying the police is something she seems to have accepted."[8] But what upset her most is that, despite the bribes to the jail wardens, Rimon did not always get the food she brought for him.

A Transparency International-Bangladesh Chapter (TI-Bangladesh) survey found that 96.3 per cent of the respondents held the police in low esteem.[9] People agreed that it was nearly impossible to get assistance from the police without financial inducement or political weight. Similarly the survey found that 73 per cent of those who had dealings with the

---

8   Alam, 2001.

9   Transparency International-Bangladesh Chapter, 2002.

judiciary had to give money to the court officials to get any work done. So getting justice in Bangladesh can be an expensive affair.

> The lives, property and way of life of the Rakhine people in the hills of Chittagong are under serious threat from the local mafia. Local musclemen have grabbed land and property through forged documents and false lawsuits, forcing many Rakhine families out of their ancestral homes and into destitution. "In one way or the other, police and local administration have always sided with the usurpers," alleged a Rakhine who was evicted from his property. For the Rakhines, the fight against this repression and injustice has been a losing battle. The systematic violence and plunder of their space and possessions has pushed many to flee the country into Myanmar.
>
> — Akter Faruk Shahin, The Daily Star, 2/8/03

The impact of such situations can be well deduced. In Rimon's case, along with his mother, he was one of the earners in the family of five, supporting the education of his younger siblings. The false arrest by the police made a poor family further destitute, in debt and emotionally shattered.

More than often, eviction of people from slums, experienced by most of the children interviewed, as well as forced ousting of minorities from their homes, also witnessed by some of the children, takes place with the compliance and collusion of law enforcement authorities and other agencies.

The poor have to pay bribes for every step they take (education, health, business). In the education sector, for example, it is very common for the majority of parents to make extra payments, such as donations (not an official requirement), to the school or use influence of the powerful for admissions. Equally, backhanded payments in the health sector for admission and care are also a regular demand by the health professionals. The TI-BC survey also reveals that 49 per cent of the respondents had to bribe municipality officials to obtain a license for a business.[10]

But some children like Shahin see the rich more vulnerable to corruption. As he puts it, "The police come and take hold of the rich people. Then they have to pay money to be released" and for this reason he prefers not to be rich.

But others are only too well aware of the menace of corruption. They argue that corruption in society contributes to their poverty. "We

---

[10] ibid.

have to pay money to get good jobs and give bribes for everything. The poor cannot afford to have political enemies or antagonise the local mafia. In the villages the *mastaans* [mafia] forcefully drive us out of our land and we end up in cities, destitute. In one village all Hindus were forced to give up their land, so they did that and moved to other villages. They had no assets left like money or property to build on. Many get cheated or robbed of their belongings as well." (Focus Group Discussion)

Although dishonest behaviour should not be justified or condoned, the reality is that the majority of Bangladeshis have incomes so low that it is impossible to survive on them, leave alone afford treats. Furthermore corruption is now so much an integral part of the system that few see it as wrong.

Rahman

I would like to be rich. But I do not know any rich people. I would have to work hard, either in service or business to be rich.

Rahman is a bright cheerful boy, who looks much younger than his age. He is a student of the literacy class. I meet him at the school after the classes are over. He is happy to talk to me about his family and his life. He is intrigued by the tape recorder and keen to see how it operates.

My name is Rahman. I am twelve-years-old. I live in Battara with my mother, father and two younger sisters. My sisters are five and three-years-old. I used to live on Road 35, till five-six months ago. The government demolished that place. We used to live in Kishoreganj. My father used to sell goats. Then three years ago he suffered a loss and then came to Dhaka.

I did not go to school, as money was needed for other things. In other schools, a fee has to be paid. From my friends I found out about the literacy class for poor children at school. I like the reading/writing part in the school (general studying). I would like to play in the school too, but there is no opportunity, time or space. I find writing most difficult, especially writing without seeing.

My mother and father help me by getting me books, by giving me food on time. It takes me ten minutes to walk to the school. I have no problem doing the homework. My parents continue to remind me. When I finish the literacy class, I will join the regular school.

It is good here in Dhaka. I know more people here. I go back sometimes to the village. People treat me very well there because I go after a long time. I need new clothes, pants and shirts-before I go back to the village. My nani (mother's mother) and my khala (mother's sister) live in Kishoreganj. My nana (maternal grandfather), and my mamu (maternal uncle) live in Sylhet. They are fruit sellers. They sell oranges and bananas.

My mother works in other people's homes. She goes in the morning at eight and comes back at four in the evening. My father has been selling tea for as long as we have been here. He goes to work at seven in the morning and comes home at one in the afternoon. He goes out again at five in the evening and is out until ten at night. He sells biscuits also. I help my father.. I look after my sisters at home when my parents are at work. I do marketing for my father; I get what he needs. Since my father comes home at 1 PM, I can go to the literacy class at 2 PM.

When I grow up, I will get a job. Or, I might do some business. I would like to be a police officer. My parents want me to do well in work and to get married.

I would like to marry when I am 20-25. Before that I would be too young, and after that too old. I would like to marry a girl who is educated and who works in an office. I would like to have two or three children. We are three children in the family, and I think that is nice.

I live in a house with a tin roof. There is a separate kitchen, there is electricity. There is a bathroom also. A tube-well is close by. I like the house because there is light, and it is an airy house. There is nothing that I do not like about the house. The locality has a play ground (khelar mat). We play football and cricket. We play two-three hours in the evening. We also watch cricket on the TV. I like Sachin Tendulkar. I like the fact that we have friends in this locality.

I get five or ten taka sometimes. I use it buy something to eat. I get biscuits.

My parents tell me not to be out of the house for long. They tell me to return home quickly. They tell me not to fight. They also warn me about bad people—those who fight and abuse others. I am afraid of being bitten by a dog, or getting an electric shock in the house. Although I have not been bitten, but my friend has.

When my parents give me something, I am very happy. I got a school bag from them. We celebrated Eid. We ate sevain (vermicelli cooked in milk and sugar), got new clothes for Eid. We sacrificed a goat and distributed the meat to others also.

I get sad when my parents fight. Sometimes when I want something and I do not get it, I become sad. Like I wanted a fan in the house but my parents did not get it. They said we could not afford it.

I like my parents and my grandparents. The person I like the most is my cousin brother, Kaka. He is educated and he is an apprentice.

I would like to be rich. But I do not know any rich people. I would have to work hard, either in service or business to be rich.

Rahman's Family

Rahman's father is a tea seller. He has a thermos flask and a few cups. He goes around looking for customers. Neither he nor his wife are educated. The ties with his family in the village exist through occasional visits to the brother who lives there. Dhaka, with its opportunities for schooling, income etc., was considered to be far better than village life.

Rahman's father would like to educate his daughter when she is the right age. Rahman's mother works in a house in Gulshan. The parents would like Rahman to study as much as he can and get into service. For the father, Rahman's doing well in school is a source of joy. Rahman's father recognises that education can draw children apart from their parents. Despite this fear, he would like Rahman to study.

Rahman's house is a 10-minute walk away from the school. A dirt path from the main road leads to a colony of houses that are built around two sides of a playground. There is a smell of cow dung and hay in the air. The houses are built in two rows. There is a narrow path that divides the two rows. Some houses are built from tin, others are made of bamboo matting. Rahman's family lives in a 7x7x8 feet room, built of bamboo matting. Cooking is done outside. When it rains, there is a common space available, where the community takes turns to cook. Water is drawn from a common tube-well. There are covered latrines, two for women and two for men. There are similar bathing places also available. When we visited, the father was at home, but the mother was away at work. There was one light bulb in the room, one bed next to the only window, about 2x1 feet in size. There was no other furniture in the house.

Rahman is one of the few boys in these stories who stays at home and looks after his siblings when his parents are away at work. His father's work schedule allows Rahman to go to the literacy classes. Rahman's story also expresses an unstated desire to look prosperous when he goes to the village. It seems migration to the city is expected to result in a better life for all.

Rahman would like to continue his education. But, if the same circumstances for his family continue, he will find it difficult to gain entry into a regular school. His story highlights the need for flexible education programmes that meet the needs of those who cannot access standard educational systems.

Mia

In the village even when you work very hard you don't get enough to eat. One can only work as a farmer. In Dhaka in comparison to 'desh' there are many opportunities.

Mia is a bright eleven-year-old, looking much younger than his age. He has not seen his father since his mother's death nine years ago. But his grandparents' love and care appear to sustain him well. Due to his injuries—sustained 17 years ago in the village—Mia's grandfather has had trouble finding work. His grandmother has been working in people's homes to support the family, but has been unable to do so for the last few months due to ill health. Their possessions are meagre. A fan, which Mia's grandmother insists on fanning me with, is a hand-made affair, a piece of cardboard (cut into fan shape) and slotted into a stick. I am a welcome visitor and the grandmother in particular wants to share her woes with me. Despite the hardships and poverty, his grandparents want to educate Mia and give him their best. It is not uncommon for them to indulge him as well.

My name is Mia. I am eleven-years-old and studying in Class III. I live in Gulshan 2—on the other side of the lake. I have lived here for four years; before this we were on Road 41. The landlord there asked us to leave. He said he would be building a house there so we had to leave. He has made a six-storey apartment block there. We lived on Road 41 for nine years. We have a house (maternal grandparents') in the village. I don't know my father; he doesn't keep in touch with us. My mother is dead. I live with my nani and nana (mother's parents). I also have my aunt and uncle (paternal) living near the airport but we don't go there. My grandparents had land in village but there was gondogol [trouble] and they had to leave and come to Dhaka. We go to the village. I would have studied there if that was possible. My nani's brother lived in the country so we go to him. He has land. I like it there. There is land there and greenery and space to play—the earth is soft. What I don't like is that there is no transport. One has to walk long distances. Besides you cannot get what you need.

In Dhaka I like everything: there is transport, there is the school which I like the best. I don't like fights and things—it happens in school and in my neighbourhood.

Nana works and nani works at home. Nana is a guard. He goes to work at night and comes back in the morning. I had a sister but she died, my mother died. I can't tell how. I was very little—a year and a half old.

My granddad can write his name but my nani has not studied. My nani is working hard for me to be educated. She says, "Study and become manush [a person]."

The house is kaccha (not solid)—with tin walls and mud floor. We have no electricity. The water is far away. It takes three to four minutes to get it. We have one room. Cooking is done outside. We have a mud stove and burn wood. The toilet is a makeshift one made of bamboo. We bathe at the tap. We are very poor. We have nothing. Once I am educated, I can become rich. So we are not rich. In my heart I feel that without education one cannot be rich.

I like school, I like studying. I have been in the school for five years, since KG. My nani wanted me to study and in my heart I want to obey my nani's desire. In my heart I know people say that I can't become a manush (person) but I will show people that my nani has educated me and made me a person. I walk from my house to the main road and take a bus from there. It takes about half an hour, but sometimes in a traffic jam it takes up to one hour. I do my homework well. My grandmother checks if I am doing my homework. She encourages me to do the homework. My grand parents can't help me as neither of them have education. In the evening I have dinner and then do the homework. I use kuppi [small kerosene lamp] for light.

I help my grandmother do the cooking, bring water. If she asks for things I fetch them. Sometimes I go to the bazaar. I get four taka per day and every week 20 taka. I have to pay two taka for bus fare, then on the days I attend music lessons (provided by the school) I spend ten taka per day for food. I get three to fours hours free when I play. I play cricket and also other games I have learnt in school.

We celebrated Eid, but not so well as I was working. I was selling balloons. This friend of mine who sells balloons asked me to help him and his dad. His father gave me ten taka. My nani agreed to this.

Once when we were going to the village someone grabbed our hen from me. My nani fought with this man and got it back. If my nani had not been there I would have lost it. Also once my nana saved me from drowning in this lake.

I want go to high school and once I finish I want to get a job or do business. Like selling balloons, or have a fruit shop, or a job like gardener or manager, like engineer. My nana and nani wish for me to get a job and become well off.

I would like to be married around 25-30 years of age. My nani would like to see my bride. I would like a poor girl, someone who will do housework. Big people are big headed. If you say something they can say you are poor we are big people. That's why I don't wish to marry a rich girl. I would like to have two children. Happy family. I don't want more. I want one girl, one boy. More, I think, I won't be able to feed and clothe and educate. If they are educated they can say namaz [prayer]. I would like my children to be educated and then I will marry them. So they are able to get a job, manage to eat, can rear children, can educate their children. I would like to have a home in Dhaka after marriage not in the village. In the village, even when you work very hard you don't get enough to eat. One can only work as a farmer. In Dhaka in comparison to desh there are many opportunities.

I really respect my nani, nana, my aunt and uncle, and my cousin. They don't beat me or ill treat me.

Rich people want to block poor people. But there are others who want the poor to be like them. But some think the poor should stay where they are—they are poor, let them be poor. Some do much work but get little pay that's why I am saying this.

Eid makes me most happy, also school outings and games give me much happiness.

Fights make me angry. My dream is to have a business or be a teacher when I grow up.

Mia's Grandfather

We are poor people. We have no assets so we came to Dhaka 17 years ago. We have had to move four times. Here we do not have to pay rent. The landlord allows us to stay free of charge. He is just waiting for the planning permission to come through for him to build his house. Then we'll have to move again. We can hardly manage from what I earn. When we start to run short, especially towards the end of the month, I ask for advance, or borrow from friends. But often we go without proper meals.

Mia's Grandmother

I have been working in people's homes all these years to make sure that we can eat and Mia can have education and become a person. He [husband] has been unable to work for over two years because of his shoulder injury. He got this job as a guard next door only a few months ago. Now I am not working due to ill health. Look at me, my hands are all weak and my body aches. If I get up, I can't sit. There is no one to look after them. He [Mia] has no mother. If I die who'll look after him. But we can't eat without work, can we?

We want Mia to finish Class V and find some work so there is someone to look after us.

I like Dhaka—it is better than the village. We have had problems—our last home was broken up, but still we get to eat more regularly. In the village sometimes we only ate once in two-three days. Here if I go to people [where she used to work] and ask, people will give something or other, even clothes, because they have plenty. In the village everyone is in the same situation, so how can they give what they don't have?

Whatever is earned goes on food and some school expenses, like bus fare and food—he says, "Oh nani I can't walk, it's so hot, I need money for bus. Oh nani I get so hungry after school I need money for snacks." I can't say no. What can I do? I tell him to start work. Saheb [head of family she worked for] says he'll give Mia work—starting from small jobs and then something good. I try to make him understand very much. I also want him to study more and get into good service. I know the benefits of education, but our need is such.

No we don't have any organisations or NGOs working here with us. If there were any I would join them, and work with them for our benefit but alone I cannot do anything.

Mia's family has already moved house five times and await eviction again any day. Though living in an environment of uncertainties and wants, Mia remains a lively young lad. His grandfather's earnings are not sufficient to sustain the family and borrowing and asking for help, especially towards the end of the month, are normal. Perhaps his spiritedness comes from the fact that he is secure in his grandparents' love. They have filled in the gap his parents left and have given him their utmost. Mia adores his grandparents, particularly his nani, and passionately desires to prove to them, and the world, that their struggle to raise him has not been in vain.

Education

Education as a necessity for survival
Education as a tool for upward mobility
Education as a distinguishing feature between those who become manus
(human being) and those who do not.

While these are some of the reasons why children and parents in these stories value education, none mentioned education as a "right of the child." It seems that what development workers, governments, and human rights activists generally consider as a right of the child, the poor and their offsprings either remain unaware, or simply do not recognise it as a right. Most children and their parents regard education as a privilege; something that has to be valued, something that is desired. Zohra puts it very eloquently when she says, "It was in my heart that my parents are not educated. If I knew how to read and write...."

Most of the parents or guardians in these stories are not educated. But all of them recognise the value of education. Ahmed's father says, "These days if you do not know how to read and write you cannot even get a guard's job." Education is something that one has to work hard to get. As Mia says, "My *nani* [maternal grandmother] is working hard for me to get educated." Other children also echo this struggle and hard work by their parents or guardians to get them educated.

Even when the parents value education, and their testimony clearly suggests that most do, one cannot assume that the children will be educated. It is estimated that only 18 per cent of the urban poor are enrolled in schools as compared to the national average of 83 per cent.[11] As with other aspects of their lives, alternative systems of education do not seem to be available to them. Family circumstances might force children out of school and into work, as it happened with Parveen. While the parents push themselves to get their children educated, in some cases siblings—more than often the older ones or girls—also make sacrifices by staying home to make way for the younger ones to go to school while the parents work. Most families that migrate from the village do not have adequate family support systems to provide alternative arrangements. This in effect means that the older siblings become the caregivers. The few day care centres that are available are unaffordable or inaccessible for families in need. As the study shows, many children in

---

11 UNICEF, *Situation Assessment and Analysis of Children and Women in Bangladesh*, December 1999.

Class Four

Teacher is Teaching and Student are Listening to her attentively.

Saidul   Saiful

the literacy class had forgone formal schooling because they were needed at home while their brothers and sisters attended school.

In cases such as Amina's, the child's income is necessary for the survival of the family. Some literature on working children suggests that the income from the child's labour might be too little to make a significant difference to the family. From these stories, however, it is obvious that the families do depend upon their children's wages, whatever it may be, for two decent meals a day. When viewed from the perspective of the planners and the policy makers, the 200 taka that Amina earns might be too meagre a sum, from the individual family's standpoint, it could make the difference between hunger/malnourishment and subsistence. Of course Amina's living with her employers is a further help for the family.

Yet vulnerability too might be defined and experienced differently by families. Parveen's family, for example, although seemingly better off, must have felt the need to pull her out of school to work in a garment factory. She too must have been under some compulsion to leave her family and try her luck in Dhaka.

While formal schools, both government and private, abound, there are not enough choices for those who cannot afford either. The private schools with their high fees and very many other demands are clearly out of the reach of the poor and the government schools, though free, do have associated costs. Uniforms, books and stationery, all have to be paid for. People who live on the bread line find these expenses difficult to bear. Most schools also tend to follow a rigid regime with no provision or accommodation for those who fall outside the so-called normal parameters. For example, there are very few schools providing formal education that take into account the needs of the poor or the working child. Thus, despite parental intentions and children's desire for education, close to one-thirds of children drop-out of the primary schools, poverty being the main reason for the high drop-out rate.[12]

Even when schooling is free, the children need help in learning well. Many children remarked that they had to walk for 30-40 minutes to get to the school. A bus ride would set the family back by 80-100 taka per month. Children need books and stationery as well. Even more importantly, they need peace and quiet to do their studies. Some children remark that they like their houses because "they can study."

---

[12] "Compulsory Primary Education, Implementation Monitoring Unit," *The Daily Star*, October 30th, 2003.

These children also have to balance between studying and helping in the house. All children, including boys, stated that they had to do household chores. Any resentment they might

In 2001, the enrolment rates for boys was 51 % as compared to 49% for girls http://www.unicef.org/bangladesh/children_355.htm

feel is rationalised: "I do all the house work as I am the older sister. Others don't do it, I have to do it. I can't be jealous of others" (Zohra).

Although both children and parents recognise the value of education for girls and boys alike, gender differences continue to exist. Parents acknowledge that in a tight situation the boys would be given preference for education over girls. This is supported by the figures at the national levels. While enrolment figures for boys and girls are equal now, the probability of girls continuing with their education is much lower. Statistics suggest that the drop-out rate is much higher for girls than boys, particularly at high school level. There are subtle ways in which support for education is denied to girls. Girls are called upon to help in the house more frequently than boys, thus leaving them less time to study. If they do not do well they are also more likely to be withdrawn from the school. Also the value of educating girls is not necessarily uniformly appreciated. In some cases, as in Parveen's, girls might be taken out, not for any obvious pressing reasons, but because they would prove more useful when earning. Educating girls is often seen as an economic liability.

Once the household chores are taken care of, there is time for schoolwork and play. Late evenings or nights are considered as convenient times for studying. Children mention the use of kerosene lamps (kuppi) to study. These lamps provide dim, localised illumination and they need to be checked constantly to make sure that sufficient oil remains. Also, they have an open flame which gets blown out easily. Very few parents can afford even a lantern, which could provide stronger and more secure light.

Children also share how their families support them in learning. Parents encourage their children to study and do well at school; they help by waking the children early in the mornings so children get ready in time; they constantly ask children and remind them about homework and are particular about discipline during exam times. Children recognise that parents cannot help them directly with their studies as most of them are not educated or have work hours that make it difficult for them to be around when children need them, but their constant encouragement and support is helpful and appreciated. Siblings also help. Ahmed says,

"My younger brother says I should do school work and he will take care of the household chores with my mother."

Children in these stories, like Bilal, say that through education they are able to "better understand things." The benefits of education go beyond learning and better prospects. There are other advantages as well. "Here I have learnt good manners, I have learnt how to behave well with others, and reading and writing," Sharmin remarks. Mia's grandmother mentions that "through schooling one becomes a *manush*." An additional difference that was visible to the researchers was the confidence level amongst children from the formal school. In both focus group discussions and individual interviews, children who were part of the regular school programme were found to be more confident and articulate. Also their knowledge base on social issues was notable. Children from the literacy class, however, were shy, hesitant, and less open to discuss issues. The formal school children were attentive, curious, and bold. When asked if they had any questions for the researchers, the children had some pertinent and probing queries. For instance, they were not at all coy about asking the authors the same question that was put to the children in the discussion groups, i.e. where on the wealth ranking scale of 1-10 would the authors place themselves.

All children indicated that they enjoyed the school, the learning and other opportunities it provides them. Children also appreciated both formal lessons as well as opportunities for creative expression. Learning, however, is not always easy. Older siblings and class teachers are the most commonly sought people to help with the difficult subjects. Nutrition is another factor that affects learning. Studies from across the world have established links between nutrition and learning. Hunger affects attention spans and makes learning more difficult. Children in these stories mention uncertainty of food

> Approximately 700 children die every day of malnutrition related causes in Bangladesh.
> — *The World Bank*

availability, and often surviving on two very basic meals a day. Malnutrition is widespread in Bangladesh. The majority of children suffer from low weight for their age and are stunted. Micro-nutrient deficiencies are also common. Both, inadequate and nutritionally deficient food puts children of the poor at an increased disadvantage for learning and succeeding.

Education is, however, not considered to be without disadvantages. Some of these are conscious and articulated, and others lie below the surface. Both create divisions in the way people view and relate to each other. Parents, particularly those who are not educated themselves, are aware of the divisive nature of education. Ahmed's father recognises that "Education will draw us (the parents and children) apart." This is a fact that they as parents must live with. Children too feel that education polishes people and makes them more of a "manush." Through schooling children acquire proper manners, which are much appreciated by adults around them. It appears that there is a belief amongst the children and the parents that only in school can one learn good conduct, and that the role of the family in propagating good behaviour and values is negligible.

A similar feeling of dissociation is evident in the rural and urban lives and people. The majority of the children consider those living in the cities to be in some sense better off. The values and the attitudes that are promoted by the schools, especially those for the poor, seem to deepen the sense of separation from the families and from rural life. The text

> "Although I had fun in the village, I like Dhaka better. There is a school here, we can learn to read and write. People talk well here."
>
> — Shahin

books commonly depict urban situations, so that children in both rural and urban areas grow up learning and valuing urban life. Appreciation of interdependence and mutual respect that an educational system can and should facilitate does not happen. Education thus often divides, rather than connects, people.

Education was unanimously considered as the pre-requisite for a better life with a view that it would open doors to many jobs. The children regard themselves as being capable of studying more and going for higher studies. For example some of them indicated that they want to be doctors. This belief in their own selves and an earnest desire to at least complete high school is tempered with an acute awareness of the limitations that poverty places on them and their future. Despite recognition, by both the parents and the children, of the need for formal education, the children in the formal school voiced their apprehensions of not being able to complete their education, or study as much as they would like to. They recognise their vulnerabilities to causes beyond their control. One case of serious illness in the family, or a loss of a job of the parent is all it would take to displace a poor child from the school into the labour force.

Amina

I live with Khala and when she respects me I do not think I am poor.

> Amina is a small built girl who looks much younger than twelve. For the interview she is wearing a pretty dress, with frills and embroidery. When the employer came to know that Amina was to meet me today, she told Amina to wear nice clothes. Her hair is oiled and combed. Amina is keen to talk to me and speaks earnestly and quickly. Her large eyes are very expressive as she describes her life and her dreams to me.

My name is Amina. I am twelve. I live on Road 35 with a woman I call Khala [Aunt]. I do household work in that house. My parents live in another house. I have been living with Khala for three years now.

I have an older sister and two younger brothers. My sister has finished Class V from a school for poor children. She now teaches in another school close to this school. One of my brothers goes to my school too. He is in Class II. It would be much nicer if I stayed with my parents. I cannot see them everyday. My sister also works, but she lives with my parents. When I go home over the weekend, then my parents are very happy to see me. My brothers and sisters are also happy to see me. My mother makes me sleep with her. My sister and brother also do special things for me.

My mother's family is from Comilla. My mamu (maternal uncle) still lives there. We go there sometimes, but not often. We went a long time ago. We do not have anything in Comilla now. My father used to be a darban [guard]. He has no job now. My parents send me to school so that I can also learn.

My [parent's] house is nice. It is built on stilts with a roof made of paper. We fill water in a big container and bring it to the house. My Khala's house, where I stay, has six rooms, fans, water, bathroom etc. I like the family I stay with. I like the things in the house. I like the furniture, but I cannot sit on it. I just see it. There is a fridge and there is a TV also. We can watch the TV after we finish work. There are chairs and mirrors in the house. There is a gas stove in the house. The house has a garden with grass, flowers pots. I like the people in the house also.

My work is difficult. I have to wash clothes. I find it difficult to wash clothes which have been used for cleaning. I fear the steps I have to climb to clean the fan. I like to sweep the garden. I do not like to wash the clothes in the winter. I like the fact that I earn. I get taka 200 per month, my mother buys food with it. Khala gives me clothes so that I look good when I come to school. Khala also gives taka four to come to the school. She encourages me to study. She gives books, pencils and enquires about school activities.

There is another girl who lives in the house. She is younger than me. I get lots of free time. She cannot read and write. Sometimes other children from the neighbourhood also call. We play with them also. I like to play in the school. There was a picnic, and there was a festival also.

I think I am poor. I live in a basti [slum]. We have to get water from far away. We cannot wash our clothes with soap. Allah made us poor. I do not know other rich people. I live with Khala and, when she respects me, I do not think I am poor. Some rich people treat me well. They tell me to come, sit, eat. I don't eat as it might get late. Some rich people don't treat well. Poor people worry that they may not get work—that is their main problem. Rich people worry about their things getting stolen.

In my house everybody does some work. My brother fetches water. He will not do girl's work. My father does the marketing. He keeps pigeons. He helps by getting wood and leaves.

I am afraid of being scolded. If work is not done properly, then I get scolded. Outside the house, many things can happen that can hurt a child; one can get run over. People also say bad things. They hit children. I do not talk to strangers as they can be bad people.

I get food and at festival time I get clothes also. I get to see my parents at festival time. I get to stay with my mother for one night. I stay with Khala for Eid. She gives me baksheesh [gift money]. I get taka 50 for Roza Eid and taka 20 for Qurbani Eid. On Eid, my brother got new clothes from my parents. Khala gave clothes for me and my sister. I also got baksheesh from my father. There was no qurbani at the house. Khala also does not do it. She is alone here, so she gives money to someone in Tongi. We got meat from the neighbours. I was happy because I got new clothes and money. We bought cakes and chips. We spent taka three on the cake. I wore new clothes.

I am sad when I do not see my mother. I like the school. When my mother does not come, I get very sad. I keep thinking why she has not come.

I would like to work in garments [garment factory]. If not garments, then I will work in a house. I would like to study further and work when I am eighteen-years-old. I do not want to get married. I want to stay with my parents. My parents too want me to stay with them.

I admire my parents, the Khala with whom I live, my siblings, my cousins and relatives. I really look upto my cousin sister . She respects me. She gives me baksheesh. She studied and then worked abroad.

I worry that I cannot see my parents or relatives; or that they may be sick. I dream that my parents have brought me back and they have bought things for my brothers and sister and me.

Amina's Family

Amina's mother is about 35 years of age. Both she and her husband are illiterate. Jamila works in a house as domestic help. Her day starts early in the morning and ends late in the evening. She gets taka 800 for the work she does. She recognises the value of education and wants all her children educated. According to her, "The poor especially need education because they have nothing else." She understands that Amina feels sad at living away from the family, but feels she has no choice. She believes that Amina is in a sensitive household where the lady of the house helps by encouraging and supporting Amina in her studies. However, Jamila was also quite clear that she would bring Amina home instead of letting her work in another house, in case the current employer left. She felt that the new employers might not be as supportive of Amina's education.

The family home is located in a slum, abutting but hidden away from the posh multi-storied buildings. The land created by filling the lake provides a dwelling area for more than 30 to 40 families. Some of the houses are built on solid land, others, like Amina's family home, are built upon stilts in the lake. The family described their fear of being blown away in a recent storm that hit the city.

The narrow 7' x 4' room is less than 4 feet in height. One has to climb steps on a flimsy ladder and crawl into the room. The room is partitioned off by a rope on which clothes are hung. This space is occupied by two adults and three children on a regular basis. All the utensils had been kept on shelves. They were all sparklingly clean. There was no other furniture nor for that matter could it have fitted in. A rope with a cloth over it provided some privacy to the family. Amina's elder sister, who came in, went behind this to change out of her clothes. Cooking is done outside on an earthen oven. Water is fetched from a tube-well some distance away. Bathing and washing are done in the lake.

Amina is one the 250,000-300,000 child domestic workers in Dhaka city.[13] She expresses the physical and psychological fears and anxieties of a working child. Her separation from her family home might have created a romantic view of the home and its environment. She describes the little one-room bamboo shack on the lake, with boats, in most poetic language.

Amina's employer is regarded in high esteem, both by Amina and her mother. The employer is very supportive of her education. Amina's mother has decided that if the lady who employs Amina leaves, she will not let Amina work any more. She is worried that the new employers might not let her study further. Despite the fact that Amina's employer is caring and supports her in many ways, the anxiety about work and separation from parents affects Amina deeply.

---

13 http://www.globalmarch.org/cl-around-the-world/little-maids-of-dhaka1.php31.

Children at Work

Sometimes I feel upset about having to work but I know that there will be no food so I manage. I do not resent it but sometimes I get very tired. I would prefer to do something easier like shop work where I can at least sit.

— Bilal

They are everywhere and nowhere—depending upon if one looks and where one looks. They can be seen in the markets, waiting to carry your heavy shopping, running to sell you flowers at traffic lights. They are also hidden away from less probing eyes in factories, in homes and brothels. It is estimated that there are 250 million working children in the world, of which 120 million work full-time. In the USA alone, more than 250,000 children, mostly under the age of 15, work illegally.[14] A study by the US General Accounting Office also reported a 250 per cent increase in child labour violations between 1983-1990.

Literature on child labour refers to working children as those who get some monetary returns for the work they do. In Bangladesh there are approximately eight million children who fall into this category. What drives these children into the labour market and what keeps them there are two sides of the same coin. Poverty, with its many causes and manifestations, is the reason cited by the majority of the working children. Besides, inadequate micro and macro level systems further continue to keep the children in the workforce and in poverty.

Why is it that so many employers are ready to hire children despite various legislations and condemnations of such a practice? While there may be many excuses and justifications, the main and obvious reason for this preference for a young workforce is inherent in the fact that the employers can get away with paying "child" wages for "adult" work. Also children are more compliant and less likely to assert themselves, making them a more manageable workforce. Of course many children also work with or for their families, in innumerable areas such as agriculture, small businesses, home enterprises, child minding and housework, thereby reducing the family's outgoings on labour.

A substantial number of these children start to work for money, or no returns, from a very early age. For seven-year-old boys it is not uncommon to be employed as helpers, street sellers, tea boys etc. Girls around this age may work as domestic servants, produce saleable items at home, and sell knick-knacks on the streets. Begging, by many, is also considered an occupation.

---

14 http://www.freethechildren.org/campaigns/cl_us.html.

More than half the children interviewed for the study have been working for a wage from an untimely age. None had a choice in the matter. Ali, in fact, left his village at the age of seven to make a living, as his mother, after his father's death, could not provide for the two of them. Amina became a live-in servant when she was nine-years-old because her parents could not sustain the family on what they earned.

> My work is difficult. I have to wash clothes. I find it difficult to wash clothes which have been used for cleaning. I fear climbing the steps I have to climb to clean the fan. I like to sweep the garden. I do not like to wash the clothes in winter. I like the fact that I earn. I get 200 taka per month, my mother buys food with it. *Khala* gives clothes so that I look good when I come to school. *Khala* also gives me four taka to go to the school. She encourages me to study. She gives books, pencils and enquires about school activities.
>
> — *Amina*

Amina is one of the few lucky ones to have a considerate employer. There are about 300,000 children employed as domestic help in Dhaka city alone.[15] Children as young as 6-7-years-old are brought from the village to work in the cities. A large number of them work more or less as bonded labours. Contact with their own families is rare, leaving these children entirely at the mercy of the employers. A twelve-hour working day is not uncommon for most of these children. Abuse, both mental and physical (and often sexual as well), is not uncommon. Severe violence towards the domestic servants is not that rare either. As many as ten cases of serious torture, rape and beatings are reported per month. In 2001 four workers between the age of seven and eighteen were reported to have been tortured to death in Dhaka. Girls and women are more at risk from such cruel treatment than boys or men.

> The 300 or so tanneries in Dhaka employ a number of children who often work 12 hours a day, seven days a week in hazardous conditions. Even after a short stint of two months in the tannery, children have complaint of headaches, nausea and skin problems. This is not surprising for very little protection is provided from harmful chemicals and acids. For working long hours, mostly in the dark, noisy putrid smelling environment a child may earn 24 taka a day. But as 13-years-old Azmal says, "I like my job because I know that it helps my family.... I would prefer to go to school. I had many friends when I was in school. Now there is no time to talk, play and laugh anymore."
>
> — *Skeem M (2002)*

---

15 http://www.globalmarch.org/cl-around-the-world/little-maids-of-dhaka1.php3.

In most industries one can find child labour. There are serious health hazards that working children face. The physical outcomes are much more visible than the psychological ones. Exposure to chemicals, working in the midst of city traffic and air and noise pollution, carrying loads beyond their physical abilities, working long hours well past what would be considered safe, are only some of the obvious causes of ill health. Even seemingly harmless activities, like sitting in one position for too long in the same place, can cause postural problems for children. The hidden psychological effects are probably even worse.

The stress of contributing to the family income and the pressure of dealing with adult demands results in anxiety, a sense of moral confusion and adult diseases. In Haragach, Bandar district alone 20,000 children below the age of 12 work in *bidi* (tobacco joints, common on the subcontinent)

> I hope someone will give me work but it does not happen. There are people who try to push us into bad [sex] work. I resist but they take me and make me do bad work. Many of the other children are in the same position.
>
> — *Ali*

factories. Many are engaged in the work from the age of seven. In return, they earn 20 taka per day and at the same time acquire susceptibility to chronic diseases such as asthma, TB, jaundice, bronchitis, kidney infection and skin and eye problems. Treatment is hardly affordable and many die young.

However, even work, as badly paid or as hard as it may be, does not come by easily. Extreme poverty forces children to live off the waste disposed by those who have more than they need or want. At least a thousand people, half of whom are children between the ages of five and fifteen, live off one of the rubbish dumps in Dhaka. Scavenging in the two-storey high waste heaps, spread across a vast area, is neither pleasant nor lucrative. The foul smelling toxic air, the rubbish full of danger (such as broken glass and sharp metal), all pose serious hazards to health. But of course there are other hazards as well. Fights, especially amongst the children, break out over who sighted something first and who has the right to it. These children work on the dumps up to eight hours a day to provide the extra income badly needed to sustain their families. There are as many girls as boys picking through the litter of the city. Often there are families (mostly new arrivals from the villages), particularly mothers and children, working the dumps, and some children have literally grown up doing this for survival. No luxury of childhood for them. No indulgences such as education, leisure activities, and celebrations for these children. The majority of them remain trapped in this impoverished work and existence.

Research in this area suggests that child labour may actually aggravate poverty in the long term, both for the family and society. Children who start work at a young age lose out on the developmental opportunities afforded through education and schooling in general. When they grow up, they face a serious disadvantage of being under-skilled and already over-extended. Studies have shown that "child workers" do not grow up to be more productive than those who were not engaged in work from an early age. Presence of child labour also depresses work opportunities for adults, contributing to unemployment and further causing child poverty.

There are many children who are out of school because they support families without being monetarily compensated for it and therefore do not appear in the statistics as "working children." Away from the eyes of the planners and policy makers, they lose out on even the few opportunities that might be available. Contrary to popular belief, the parents in these stories would much rather see their children in school than have them work for money. It is lack of opportunities for the adults to earn a living, or sufficient wages to meet the needs of their families, that keeps their children out of school and in the labour market.

Bangladesh, together with other South Asian countries has adopted the Rawalpindi Resolution (Pakistan, 1996), which aimed to abolish hazardous child labour by the year 2000, and all forms of child labour by 2010.[16] Needless to say, the year 2000 has come and gone, and not much has been done to prevent child labour in hazardous industries. It is also clear that child labour is a reality that has no easy or short-term solutions.

---

[16] http://www.sdnpbd.org/sdi/international_day/childrens_day/ipec.htm.

Sarmin

Rich people look down on the poor. They look at our clothes and find them dirty and smelly. They are repulsed by us. But we do not have many clothes, we can't wash our clothes every day.

I meet Sarmin at the school and walk with her to the house. She points out the rubbish overflowing in the gutters and the stagnant water around her house. Sarmin's whole family, except her father, are there to greet me. They all are worried as to where I can sit as there is no space in their tiny room.

Sarmin's grievance goes much beyond her impoverished living conditions. She is frustrated with the complete lack of care displayed by her neighbours to cleanliness in the *basti*. She is wise enough to perceive that some things, which at least could be better and have little to do with poverty, are wilfully ignored by people.

My name is Sarmin, I am ten-years-old. I live in a basti near my school. We have lived there for ten years. We do not have a house in the village. In my house I have my three brothers, me and my younger sister. One brother studies in this school, one is at home and another does small jobs-some business.

My father is a rickshaw puller and my mother does house work. My parents have no education. My big brother has studied. He can do maths. We are poor people. Many of us live in one small room. We do not get enough to eat. We live in the slum in one room. Our cooking is done just outside. We have no running water in the house. We have to bring the water from outside. Our toilet is by the lake—a shelter has been erected—and we have our bath in the lake water. Our slum is very dirty. People just throw things anywhere and everywhere. The thing I like about my neighbourhood is that I can play around. What I don't like is that you can't tell anyone to keep the place clean.

My parents wanted me to go to school. I know that if I get education I can get many jobs, good jobs. I like doing studies in school and they give us food. My brother helps me with the homework.

I help my mother to cook. Sometimes I cook, look after my little sister, clean the house. Sometimes if my mother is busy or out, I keep the baby. My brother who is at home does help. He brings water, sometimes he cooks. I don't get pocket money. I don't need it. Sometimes if I want something, I ask my mother and she gets it for me.

I have one or two hours free time. Then I play with my friends. My friends are all from this area. None of the children from my school live here. My friends are all girls, but we also play with smaller boys. We do skipping, hop-scotch, five stones and many more. My parents do not allow me to play with bad children, those who do not listen to their parents even when they get told off, don't do the work when asked by their mothers.

Where I live there are rich people nearby. There is a five-storey building with flats. They treat us well. When they see us [the children] they say, "How are you" and "Let's play." We play together sometimes. I am afraid of traffic on the roads. I could get hit. My parents warn me against bad children, and I say I won't be like them.

For me, the happiest time is when I pass my exams or win in games. It is like a prize.

We celebrated Eid. Got new clothes, went to my aunt's house, and different friends and family came to our house at night. It made me very happy. We also celebrated 'Ekushe February' (21st February, the National Language Day). We decorated the place with many things.

My little sister had a serious accident. We were all distressed. We had no money for treatment. My father had to borrow some.

I have many wishes for when I grow up, but we are poor and they will not be fulfilled.

I want to continue with my studies and become a doctor. I don't know what my parents wish for me. They haven't said. My parents will arrange my marriage. I would like to get married when I am 25. I want to have two children. More children need more money and it won't be possible to manage. I want to marry someone who is better educated than me. If I can't manage something, he will be able to. I don't think early marriage (15-16) is right. The girl can become pregnant, and can have complications and other problems. I have seen it in my village. Also my mother has said things.

I respect my mother. She is very good. She manages everything. She allows me to play and gives me freedom. My father is strict. I admire my aunty. I want to be like her. She works—I don't know what job, but she is educated. She has studied up to Class V and used to work for a garment factory. That job is now no more, and she is looking for another. I will study if my mother asks me to study or work if she so wants. Working as a teacher, or in the garment industry, or working in an office.

Rich people look down on the poor. They look at our clothes and find them dirty and smelly. They are repulsed by us. But we do not have many clothes, and we can't wash our clothes every day.

If I become rich it will be good. I could win a lottery, or do some business. Some people do bad things, bad business. I won't do that. In our house we don't have three meals. Sometimes not even two. It upsets me very much. My dream is to be a doctor.

Sarmin's Mother

My husband is a rickshaw puller. My two boys work in the garment industry, two children are in school, and the last one is just two-years-old. Even with three incomes we are always short—their incomes are not much. One earns 500 and one 700 taka per month. My husband brings in different amounts— average 35-50 taka per day. Since the closure of main roads to rickshaws, he has to pull double the time for the same journeys, so his income has halved. The major amount goes on the rent—650 taka per month. We need roughly 100 taka per day for basic meals. We sometimes borrow. We don't have a family to fall back upon. We buy clothes may be twice or thrice a year. We spent about 1000 taka at Eid time to buy shoes etc.

My husband does not have any land or assets, so we manage with what they earn. We do not have any savings. There are no organisations or NGOs in my area—not that I know of. I do not vote here as I am registered in the previous area. One of the boys is educated up to Class II and the other to Class III. I would like the other two to study as much as possible, circumstances permitting.

Sarmin's parents' own lack of education makes them even more determined to send their children to school at a great cost and sacrifice to themselves. But her father cannot make a living wage as a rickshaw puller, so two of the sons, age 15 and 13, had to give up their studies and start working. The family needs only 100 taka a day for food. Yet even with three family members working this seems impossible.

Sarmin may look younger than ten, but she is wiser than her age. She understands the consequences of poverty and the limitations it puts upon her parents and her own future. She dreams of being a doctor but is aware that she may have to accept much less than that.

Behaviour of the Rich Towards the Poor

Our next-door neighbour has a television. It looks very nice. It is quite a large one. Generally the rich people buy televisions. The rich do not allow the poor to enter their houses to watch TV. We are poor, so what! Should we also not deserve or desire to watch TV? Not only the rich neighbours, but also most of the rich people neglect the poor. They don't allow their children to play with the slum children.

— Begum, age 10

Poor children become aware of the differences between themselves and the wealthy at an early age. The group discussion with the kindergarten children in fact shows how early it is in life that the meaning of "rich" and "poor" and the value of money are perceived and appreciated by the children. This awareness is accompanied by a comprehension of subtle nuances that characterise the attitudes of the rich and their interaction with the poor. Not all children have had direct contact with a rich person, or know one. But observations and limited experience (including experience of adults in family) has made the children aware of the differences between the rich and the poor.

All the same the children recognise that not all rich people are alike. They also seem to recognise an inherent risk in generalising all rich people in the same way. According to the children, some rich people treat the poor well. These people seem genuinely interested in the lives of the poor. By their behaviour and their questions these people communicate this interest to the children and their families. Then there are others who look down upon the poor. Children sense this and are extremely hurt by this.

> There is no way we can predict how someone is going to behave. People are different and they behave differently. There are some who treat us well and there are others who don't. Even within a family, some members behave well and others don't.
>
> *— Focus Group Discussion Class IV*

For the children appearance is the most distinguishing characteristic of the poor. They seem to sense the negative reaction of the rich to their outer shell. From the children's perspective, the rich do not have the sensitivity to realise that the poor dress the way they do because they cannot afford any better. If the rich were to understand that soap is a luxury, they would know why poor people smell. Even in friendship, the rich seem to be unaware of how lack of funds affects the lives of the poor. One of the children narrates how a rich friend shouts and gets angry when he is late and expects him to come by rickshaw to be on time. The rich boy does not realise that spending even a few taka on transport is not an option for the poor.

Most of the interaction between the rich and the poor seems to be in the work situation. Beneath the seemingly neutral and outwardly calm relationship, there are tensions lurking under the surface. The employer-employee relationship, especially in the informal sector of domestic help, is fraught with difficulties. The nature of the relationship itself seems to swing between the traditional master-servant arrangement of the feudal years where the employers would take care of the servant for life and the present-day contractual agreements. This lack of clarity could be one of the causes of hidden expectations and lack of trust. The rich, it appears, do not have the sensitivity to identify genuine need and behave accordingly. Cases of termination of employment due to unexpected or extended leave are common. The poor children in these stories do not understand why the rich employers cannot give an advance on the salaries when they need it. It also seems that rich parents find it quite acceptable for their children to shout at and be demanding of the household help, irrespective of the employee's age, and affirm their role as the "master of the house."

The children also find it difficult to comprehend the priorities of the rich. They are bewildered by the principles that govern the actions of the rich people. It is inexplicable to

> "The boss was going to give two sets of clothes, but madam said let's us give only one now and give the second for next Eid."
> — *Focus Group Discussion*

them that the rich can feed their dogs and look after them and not give something to the poor. Or, when the employer can afford to, or is willing to, give then why do they need to wait until the next festival.

Even in extremely supportive relationships, as Amina has with her employer, there are clear boundaries between what she can and cannot do. She can clean the furniture but she cannot sit on it. These boundaries might change because she is a child of 12, but perhaps only to a limited extent. For most of the part, the child is treated the same as an adult, both in terms of work, as well as behavioural expectations. Age does not appear to affect the relationship between the employer and the

> "Around us there are people with more money than us and also with less. The ones richer than us have TV. Sometimes I like to go and watch TV there but they don't let me. When their children come to play sometimes I don't play with them as I feel hurt."
> — *Zohra*

employee. Some children in these stories live in close proximity to the rich. The bamboo or mud shacks of the poor adjoin the multi-storeyed houses of the rich. This shared space also means closer interaction between the children of the rich and the poor. Not all rich people like their children to play with poor children. There are others whose children do play with poor children. This interaction from the children's account seems to be controlled by the rich. While the rich children can come and play with the poor in their neighbourhood, the poor or their children do not have the same access to the rich or their homes. The children sense this inequality and resent it.

The rich can either facilitate or hinder a poor person's progress. Some rich people are considered to be helpful towards the poor. They actively work towards the betterment of the poor. Amina's employer is one of these. She not only supports Amina's education but also encourages her to study. She is considered, however, one of a kind. Not all rich people are thought of as so positively inclined as to help the poor. There are others who are seen actively preventing the progress of the poor. Cases of

> Rich people want to block poor people. But there are others who want the poor to be like them. But some think the poor should stay where they are— they are poor let them be poor. Some do much work but get little pay that's why I am saying this.
>
> — Mia

exploitation are common. In fact, the salaries that are given to young children or adults for work in the domestic sector are shocking. Children recognise and resent this exploitation. However, they also recognise that jobs, especially in considerate households, are rare.

From what the children say, it appears that the rich judge the poor by what they have and how they look, rather than what they are capable of. Children feel that the wealthy behave badly whether they are in the village or in the cities. They feel that in the shops also they get treated badly because they are poor. Some rich people, according to the children, do not even look at the poor people, giving the impression that by not acknowledging the poor they can wish them away.

> People do look down on us poor. They do not recognise us as human beings. The police harass us the most, day and night. They beat us, kick us, wake us up and take us to the police station.
>
> — Ali

Poor children are able to differentiate between charity and equality. They recognise and appreciate respect when they get it. When the rich give the same food they themselves eat to the poor, it is deemed as a sign of respect. In fact respect for some children can compensate for the lack of wealth. As Amina says, "When Auntie respects me, I forget I am poor." Respect is an integral part of human dignity and, for these children, it transpires, is the only factor that can to some extent redeem the inequalities that permeate the lives of the poor.

> In reality the friend of a poor person is another poor person. A rich person cannot be a friend of the poor. They think that if their children play with us they will be spoilt by our touch.
>
> — Sanwar

Despite attempts by the poor children not to generalise about the rich and their behaviour, the majority of interactions obviously affirm their belief that the rich look down upon the poor. Only if the rich were to make an attempt to know how the poor live, would they be able to appreciate the effort of survival under severely constrained circumstances. This would, of course, require willingness on the part of those who have never had to experience such limitations. The rich also need to acknowledge that the poor provide the support system through which they, the rich, are able to pursue a lifestyle that would not be possible otherwise. Whether it is the domestic help or the rickshaw puller, their services are the backbones on which other more profitable ventures develop. This recognition and appreciation is critical to the development of an equal and a fair society. It is also clear that this process will take time. In the interim, there is one small step that can help offset to some extent the inequalities: respect for the people and restoring human dignity (the two most deep-seated basic human needs) could well be a starting point for redressing the imbalances.

> Study by Gaag in UK amongst people living in poverty concludes that most of the people in the study felt that people ought to be respected for what they are and not what they have. "The need for respect comes high on the list of all those experiencing poverty." Some of the people interviewed strongly argued that the major misfortune for human beings is not hunger or illiteracy or even lack of work: "The greatest misfortune of all is that you count for nothing."
>
> — Gaag, 1999

For many living in poverty means not only worrying about the next meal but also putting up with the scorn and disdain of the better off. As a consequence they end up with a sense of alienation and disempowerment— a damaged spirit.

CHAPTER 4

OUR THOUGHTS, OUR OBSERVATIONS
AND OUR HOPES

What is poverty?
What does it mean to be poor and what does it mean to be rich?
How are girls and boys treated in the families?
How does wealth affect the parent-child relationship?
How does poverty affect future aspirations?
What are their future plans?
What would you like Bangladesh to be?
What kind of a world would you like to live in?

Children's thoughts on the above questions show how they view their lives, how their lives are woven with those of the rich, and how local conditions are being shaped by global events. On grounds of privacy and ethics, there were initial reservations about exploring in an open forum topics that affected the children's personal and immediate lives and severely restricted their opportunities to grow and develop in the future. The first focus group discussion with the children, however, proved that these fears were unwarranted. The children displayed enthusiasm for this rare opportunity where outsiders were interested in their lives, their feelings and their plans. The topics for discussion took the children into previously unexplored areas of personal, national and international interests. The poverty of material wealth has by no means led to poverty of hope and desire—home and desire not just for themselves but for the country and the world as well. Nor has it led to poverty of mind. Children as young as four-years-old show a keen awareness of what it means to be poor, and how poverty affects their lives.

In this chapter the children describe what the term poverty means to them and how it affects their lives. Through focus group discussions

140 children share their lives of deprivation, their views on the value of money and express their concerns on some pertinent national and international issues. The children analyse the lives of the rich and furnish causes for the disparity between the wealthy and the poor and articulate their hopes for their own future and for their nation, Bangladesh. The children conclude their deliberations and analysis with some solutions to poverty, their own roles and responsibilities to this end and that of the state.

All efforts have been made to present the children's views in their words.

Poverty: As Defined by the Children

Without a doubt children from a very young age are well aware of the poverty they live in and that is around them. All the children who participated saw themselves as poor, albeit in varying degrees.

Poverty for most means, as very simply defined by 11-year-old Shumita, "immense want of five basic needs of human beings which are food, shelter, clothes, education and medicine." The non-fulfilment of one or more of these basic needs, through lack of money, land, job, is seen as being poor and Shumita suggests, "the poor always live in want of one or more of the basic needs."

In other words not having what one needs for survival spells poverty.

Poverty—Meaning, Causes and Effects:
As Voiced by the Children

We think being poor means having certain things and not having others. Those people who have no money, who do not have enough to eat are poor. You can recognise poor people by their appearance. Their clothes are dirty and torn. There are some people who do not have houses. When the poor do have houses, these are likely to be made of tin, bamboo, mud and paper. Some poor people live on the streets. The homes of the poor do not have much furniture.

But, that does not mean the poor have nothing. The poor have some things that are unique to them, those that the rich people do not have. The poor have peace of mind. When the poor sleep at night, they sleep peacefully. They have a much stronger connection with the village and the rural life than rich people do. The poor have love and affection. They have mother's love. The poor are also always ready to help others like themselves because they know what it means to be poor.

Poverty means worries, worries about survival, about getting a job, about feeding their children, about not having money, not having a house... there are so many things that the poor live in want of. These worries are with them every day. Some poor people live in other people's homes or on their land. They can be asked to leave any time. "Some of us have moved houses many times. In some cases our houses were broken by the government. A few of us had to leave because the landlord wanted the plot back." Poor children have many worries too. "We worry what will happen if our fathers cannot get three meals for us. We also think about what we can do to help our parents. Many of us think if we could get a job, we would be able to help our parents. We also think about how we can save." Girls also worry about getting a good husband and getting married in a good family.

But, even with all these worries, the poor have fewer worries than the rich. The rich have so much more to lose so they worry more. They will also find deprivation harder and adjustment more difficult.

Most poor people are farmers, day labourers and rickshaw pullers. Some of them do building work. Others can do skilled work like cobblers, masons, carpenters. There are some poor people with their own business like the tea sellers. There are some highly skilled people like teachers and nurses who are also poor.

The poor are concerned about the future of their children. They want their children to do well in their studies. They want their children to have a good future. The poor worry about how their children will grow up. "Our parents are constantly telling us to be careful of the bad elements in the society. They tell us to be careful of those who are addicted to alcohol or drugs. The parents tell us girls to stay close to the household, not to talk to strangers. Our parents advise us to study well. They caution us on possible risks, particularly on dangers of going to areas where the *mastaans* live. On *hartal* days, our parents tell us not to play on the streets." Girls are told not to talk to boys. "We are also warned about talking to bad boys and girls." Boys are also told not to talk to bad girls—girls who talk to everyone are those who have bad conduct. Bad boys drink, take drugs, throw acid. "One of us has an uncle who had acid thrown on him."

There is no one single cause of poverty. It seems that almost always the poor are poor because of reasons beyond their control. Some are poor because they cannot get jobs. They do not get jobs because they do not have skills requisite. In some cases, there is no demand for the skills that people have. The market could have changed and there is no need for the skills they have acquired. Many poor people have no education and without it they get cheated. Sometimes they suffer a loss in business which leads to more problems. In the villages people are poor because they have no land, and they are not educated.

People also become poor because they get exploited by more powerful people like the *mastaans*. Some communities, like the minorities, are more likely to be exploited by the powerful people. In one village, all the Hindus had to leave because the powerful local people threatened them.

Exploitation is also a reason for poverty and widening of the gap between the rich and the poor. Some rich people buy things from the poor at low prices and then sell them off for a high profit. So the rich end up making the money. The poor work hard for less money and the rich work less for more money. And because the poor people are uneducated, they do not understand and get cheated.

Some people are more vulnerable and therefore likely to become poor. Those who have assets like property, money in the bank which they can use, and make more are less likely to become poor. "Even one event in our lives can lead to poverty." If a poor man has to get his daughter married, he sells off everything for dowry. If there is no dowry then there will be violence in the family. This happens amongst the rich too, but to a lesser extent. There is also vulnerability to natural disasters; for instance some people lose their land to floods.

"Our science book tells us that high population leads to poverty. As the number of people increases, the amount of cultivable land decreases. We have also seen that in many poor families there is only one earning member and too many dependents." It is also not possible for such a large population to be educated. Poor uneducated parents cannot help their children to become educated or better off.

The government of each country is responsible for everything, including poverty. The government in our country mismanages. Many people do not pay taxes. The government also does not distribute income properly.

But We Believe Poverty Is Not Destiny

Everybody is responsible for his or her own self. If we try to become big we will. If people try they can become better. If people do not study and spend everything then they too will become poor. If we work well then we will become better.

There are very few amongst us who think that poverty is due to fate and that fate cannot be changed. Nor do many of us believe that people are poor because Allah made them poor.

Life of the Rich: Children's Observations and Experiences

There are many differences between the rich and the poor. We observe people, we read books and we have seen rich people in our own families. Sometimes we go to the homes where our parents work and see how the rich live. We have also observed people on the streets and seen the rich people who live in our neighbourhoods. That is how we have come to know that there are differences between the rich and the poor.

The rich seem to have everything. The rich have cars, they have houses and factories and offices. The houses of the rich are located in wealthy neighbourhoods. Because of their location, the rich also have good neighbours. Their houses are well equipped with furniture, TV, fans, air-conditioners. There are some things that rich people will not have. They will not have rickshaws or broken chairs and tables in their homes. The rich people have servants in their houses to help with chores.

One can make out the rich by their appearance and their demeanour. Their clothes are well made. They also conduct themselves differently. The rich keep themselves aloof; they mingle only with the rich. They speak in English and even swear in English. You will not see rich people fighting on the streets. They behave well with everyone. Some rich people help the poor. The rich value respect, love and good character.

The rich have choices. They can eat what they want, when they want. They have a variety of food to choose from: Chinese, roasts, foreign food and fruits. They do as they please. They can go abroad when they want.

They might have money, but they have no peace. It seems that they are always worried about money—how to make money, how to save money and how to spend it and how to protect it from being stolen. This constant need to make more money is with them even when they are eating. We think rich people are also less able to adjust to circumstances. They are so used to living in a certain way, with comforts, that any change affects them a lot. Whereas the poor are used to living with uncertainty. The rich cannot do manual labour. The rich are more at risk than the poor, as they have more to lose. They will find the adjustments to poverty more difficult.

Rich parents tell their children not to play with poor kids. They also warn them about taking drugs and alcohol. The children are also told not to behave badly in clubs. The rich parents are also worried about the safety of their children. They tell their children to only go out in the car with the driver]. Rich girls are also told not to go out too much. Rich parents show their love by providing for their children. They are able to take care of their children. The rich respect their children; they give their children the food they want, and the toys they want and send them for education abroad.

The parents worry about what will happen if the children become spoilt and follow the wrong path. Sometimes there is a breakdown in parent-child communication. It seems that the rich want more and more for their children. The children also want to be more successful than their parents. Girls from well-to-do families worry about getting good husbands and think about giving their children a good education. If girls are educated they worry about getting a husband who is better educated than them. Children also want different things than their parents. If the parents are happy with Bangladeshi food, the children want Chinese food—they put pressure on their parents for things.

The rich can get out of trouble because of money and connections. They will not mend their own car if the car breaks down—they need someone else to mend it for them. The rich will feed their dogs but not the poor.

The rich are rich because they are educated. Without education we will not know what we need to do and how. They have good jobs or businesses. The rich are also well qualified so they can get good jobs. They are engineers, doctors or officers.

There are inequalities in the world. The way the world works is not fair. The poor work hard and get less; the rich work less and get more. There are rich people who become rich by exploiting and using the poor. The rich are also able to use their intelligence to get richer. The rich are able to save; they have money in the bank, which makes more money for them.

"How Can Poverty Be Reduced?"

When it comes to the question of how poverty in Bangladesh can be reduced, the children are neither lacking in ideas nor in fortitude. They are fully aware of the fact that causes of poverty are manifold and thus the solutions also lie in many areas. The general opinion is that efforts are required on the part of all Bangladeshis, including themselves, to reduce poverty and bring about in changes society.

Education is one of the areas that all children identified as a key factor in helping pull the poor out of poverty. They argued that without education it is difficult for individuals to know what to do and how to do it. But at the same time they were wise enough to pinpoint other elements that are equally important to tackle poverty. Having small families and doing hard work, for example, are also considered crucial to deal with poverty.

The size of the Bangladesh population is seen as a major contributor to the country's poverty and as a hurdle to change. The children propose a joint effort to challenge this issue: while the people need to learn to have fewer children, the government also has to help bring about this understanding.

However, responsibility is also put on the government's shoulder for creation of poverty, as it is the body in charge of running the nation. It was argued that the government projects do not include the real needy. Thus the onus was put on the government to provide care for the poor and helpless in a planned way. The expectation is that the government ought to set up projects that will "help the poor to help themselves." At the same time it was maintained that, unless people were vigilant and kept a check on the government, little would change.

The children argue that the poor also need support from the rich to achieve some of the goals like education and employment. They suggest that the rich could give land to the landless poor to work on, on a temporary basis. And after the poor had made some profits out of the land, they could return it to the donor. Also, if needed the wealthy could give money to the needy, thus setting a good example for others to follow.

Getting better-paid jobs is also considered a way out of the poverty trap.

The dominant view is that hard work and education are the main components that will help uplift people out of poverty. None were apprehensive of hard work, which included starting up business, going abroad to work and finding gainful employment within the country. But support from abroad was not ruled out. It was suggested that people from rich countries could help with money, or perhaps, they could help the poor buy businesses rather than give money. This would help others into employment as well, it was suggested.

The children also argued that the poor should try to save rather than fritter away their earnings.

Surprisingly enough, of the 140 children who participated in the focus group discussions, only two mentioned God in relation to reducing poverty. Despite growing up in a religious environment, the children do not show any signs of fatalism. They would like to stand on their own feet and are prepared to work hard, and put in all efforts needed to make their life and society better. But they also believe that support is needed from different quarters to give the poor a lift.

The children strongly believe that unless all people in the country are prepared to work hard and work together, the situation will not improve for, ultimately, they argue, "self help is the best help."

"Our Hopes for Our Future"

Children in these stories describe what it means to be poor and live in conditions deprived of basic facilities. They narrate what it denotes for them to be in school and how learning is essential to success, and what they want from their future, both for self as well as for the world. Out of these stories and discussions emerges a quiet confidence in their own future. Children do not indicate any major fears or apprehensions about their prospects. If there are any fears, they have to do with the loss of a parent and the resultant insecurity. Zohra, the 13-year-old, says, "I am not much afraid about the future. But if my mother is ill I get very afraid. I worry if she dies what will I do—if my father is not there and it is night time and no one can come to help what will I do?" Other children too are positive about the future. There is an inherent belief that the future will be good. This belief seems to stem from the resilience of the human spirit; a belief that is not tempered by the depressive conditions the children are growing up in. Shahin remarks about his future: "*Bhalo he hobe*" (It will be good).

> In ancient days women were not permitted to go out of their homes. They did not have the opportunity for education. Then men used to torture women. The condition of illiterate women was dire. But now the situation has changed. Women have learnt to stand on their own feet. Our Prime Minister is also a woman. So I don't want to be a timid woman in society and that is why I am studying at school.
>
> — *Saima*

The children have given certain thought to their life ahead. Some think about it in greater detail and others have painted it with much broader brush strokes. Most of the children indicate their desire to continue with their studies. Even Parveen, the girl who lives on the streets, wishes that she had continued with her education. The children in

> It will not be possible for me to do studies. I will have to work in someone's house. I would like to study further and do better.
>
> — *Zohra*

school want to complete at least primary level education, and some want to go on to the secondary schools. A few would like to complete high school as well. Their desire for education beyond the primary level, most feel, will probably remain an unfulfilled dream.

Secondary education, unlike primary education in Bangladesh, is not state subsidised. There are programmes for providing stipends for girls to continue in secondary level at the government schools. These programmes are generally considered successful in keeping girls in school. However, the government schools are mainly formal institutions, where schooling cannot be pursued with other activities. Non-formal education that offers flexible approaches is rare, particularly for urban Bangladesh. For families where every earning hand is crucial for continued existence, pursuit of further education, despite incentives would be a luxury. So while the children and their parents would like education to continue, their existing resources would not be able to support any such desires.

Children, poor or rich, have ambitions and dreams. While poverty might subdue ambition, it does not seem to constrict dreams. Children want to become doctors, singers or police officers. The difference between the rich and the poor lies in the abilities to translate the dreams into reality. These children are extremely conscious of the fact that they would be unable to realise their dreams. They are aware that studying medicine requires not only many years of education and money, but it

> I have many wishes for when I grow up but we are poor and they will not be fulfilled. I want to continue with my studies and be a doctor. I don't know what my parents wish for me.
>
> — *Sarmin*

also means loss of one person's earnings for those many years. For many of them even the modest ambitions of being a bus conductor or a driver are going to be difficult to achieve.

Given the unchanging economic reality of their situations, and the absence of suitable educational programmes for working children, most children are acutely aware that after primary school it will be time for them to get a job to support their families. For some children there seems to be a disconnection between the desire to complete higher education and the type of jobs that they would like to do. For instance, Rahman wants to go in for higher studies. But when asked about the job that he would like to do, he indicates that he wants to be a gardener or a guard. Perhaps it is desire being stifled by reality.

Jobs are not easy to come by. Unemployment in Bangladesh is high. According to the Human Development Report, unemployment amongst youth aged 15-24 has risen from three per cent in 1990 to eleven per cent in 2001.[17] The children recognise that it is going to be difficult for them to get good jobs without help. Ali, the street-child, says that often he has been promised a job, only to be led into doing "bad things."

> In truth I would like to get a job but that is not going to be easy as for jobs first you need money to bribe. So I want to do fish business because I can go to the river, catch fish and sell them.
>
> — Mohammad

The desire to be independent is strong in all the children. As Parveen, says, "I want to stand on my own feet." The children's future plans are constructed upon their present conditions and the opportunities that seem to be available for them. The girls want to work in the garment industry or in homes as domestic help, possibly because these are the most visible forms of employment in cities for women from a poor background. It is estimated that 81 per cent of the women contribute towards family earnings in Bangladesh. Nevertheless, women's participation in business and industry remains limited.[18] Boys want to be drivers, policemen, or guards. With each type of a job there is a particular image that makes it desirable. The guard opens the gates and lets the cars in... it is this aspect of "control" that makes it a job to aspire for. Some boys consider having their own business as an alternative. While luck is recognised as a critical determinant to success, the awareness that bribes, influence and financial support are needed for businesses as well has not appeared to have developed as yet for some.

The children in their stories do not indicate a desire to be very rich. They are aware that from the point they are at much hard work is needed for

> I want a nice house after I am married—somewhere clean and peaceful. Yes I want to be rich but wanting something does not mean one gets it.
>
> — Zohra

---

17 United Nations Development Programme, 2003.
18 Mahbub ul Haq, 2001.

them to become wealthy. It seems as if the reality of their situation is already tempering their ambitions and desires.

The children want a life that is better off than what it is at present. With the exception of a couple of the children, most (in the group discussions as well) prefer a comfortable life—an existence that is an improvement on their present conditions. A more secure future, in which the house is rented and not a makeshift job on illegally occupied land, is what someone like Farida wishes for. Less noisy and cleaner living conditions are what most of them dream of. When asked to identify where they would like to be on a scale of 1-10, with ten being the wealthiest, most children expressed a desire to be situated between points 5 to 7. This position, they believe, would allow them a life of comfort and peace of mind.

There is recognition that being wealthy is not without its problems, although of a different kind to those of the poor. Many children remark that the rich do not have peace of mind. The children feel that the rich are at the risk of losing more as they have more to lose. Wealth is accompanied with its own set of worries of protecting existing wealth, making more and desiring even more for their own children. The wealth that provides them with comforts and luxuries also makes the rich easy targets for extortion.

> I would not want to be rich. The police come and take hold of the rich people. Then they have to pay money to be released. The police take away rich/good people. They leave the poor people. This happens where I live.
>
> — Shahin

The children have clearly given some thought to their personal lives. Both the age of marriage and the prospective partners have been considered carefully. One child was definite that she did not want to get married. Her only desire was to come back and live with her parents. Zohra also does not want to get married but recognises that marriage is inevitable. She says, "I do not wish to marry now or when I am 25. But marriage will happen. As I grow older, if I am not married people will talk 'the girl is so big and they are not getting her married'. But how can one get married without meeting the demands [of dowry]?" Most of the children consider around 20 to 30 as an appropriate age for marriage. While the legal age for marriage in Bangladesh is 18 for women and 21 for men, in cities women tend to marry at a later age—25 to 30 is not uncommon. The children are aware of the legal marriage age and do not deem early wedlock as acceptable. Some girls are also conscious of the physical complications of an early marriage. The boys would like to get married to an educated girl. Good families are considered essential for the match. Some children specify that they would like a girl who knows Arabic and so is able to read the Quran. Boys also mention that they would not like to marry a girl from a rich family, as adjustment would be easier if backgrounds were similar.

> I would like to marry when I am grown up, when I am 20. I would like the girl to be beautiful and educated—someone who can read Arabic. It is the language of our religion. I know Arabic. I want her to be from a small family and not very rich. She can adjust better in a poor environment if she is from the same background.
>
> — Muhammad

Girls also seem to be clear about their life partners. They would like to marry someone who has a good job and treats women well. A non-smoker and non-drinker were other qualities that were specified. Both girls and boys who mentioned the issue of dowry were very much against it. One girl was quite specific that she would not like to get married to someone who demanded dowry "or other things." There was also recognition that finding a partner without the dowry would be

> I would like to marry a person who speaks well to women. Someone who does not fight. He should have a good job in an office.
>
> — Farida

difficult. The girls, like the boys, did not want to get married to anyone richer than themselves. Both girls and boys wanted to get married to an educated person. Girls, preferred boys more educated than themselves.

> My dream is to be a good cricketer. But my parents don't want me to be the same. They want me to be a service holder in future. My second dream is to be a good singer but that is also not approved by my parents. My parents do not respect my desires and dreams of the future. When I become a man and a father, I will not ignore my children's desires and wishes. I will respect their likes and dislikes. The behaviour of my parents is not parental behaviour. I will not do the same with my children. I think they are doing all these things because they are not educated. I want all parents to be educated so that their children may have proper guidance.
>
> — Saleem, age 11

Most of the children wanted to have not more than two or three children. Only one girl indicated that she wanted just one child—a boy, as boys can work outside the house. Smaller families are considered more affordable and desirable. Certainly educating their children is considered a priority by all.

Within the parameters set by reality and ability, the children see future progress for themselves and their families. Almost all children feel capable of providing a better future for their children. As they hope for progress for themselves and their families, the children also envisage a more prosperous Bangladesh. They dream of a country where there is no hunger and no poverty, a country where there is no terrorism and where peace prevails. Girls wish for a society that respects women, where there is no abuse of women. Education for all, the children believe, will lead to progress and prosperity. They believe that if the Government works properly, Bangladesh can once again become *Sonar Bangla* (Golden Bangladesh).

CHAPTER 5

THE BIGGER PICTURE

One thing the children's stories show is that people living in poverty are not the cause of it, they are the victims. They tell us of the circumstances that have contributed to, and continue to add to their own family's poor existence. Through these stories it is also possible to trace the roots and the web of poverty. The descent into poverty has been either a gradual one, with a slow depletion of resources as in Ahmed's case, or like Ali's, precipitated by a critical event such as illness or death in the family. The families do not have adequate resources, material or human, nor do they have the support systems to bear these calamitous events. Lack of food, unhygienic conditions, hard physical labour affect the health of the poor and their productivity, setting into motion the vicious cycle of low income and continued or worsened poverty.

In Bangladesh, frequent natural disasters such as floods, cyclones and tornadoes end up claiming lives, land and fortunes. Break-up of large family holdings and inadequate employment possibilities are resulting in an increase in the number of people to be supported by a smaller land size. Lack of adequate health systems, educational and economic opportunities further add to the "push" factor, drawing people to the cities. The cities provide work but are not equipped with the infrastructure to provide humane living conditions for the daily influx of population. It is estimated that with the current flow of people from rural areas into the cities, the population of Dhaka will double by 2030, reaching over 22 million. Already the poverty levels are higher in the cities. With such an influx and little in place to support the inflow, the poverty levels are expected to rise dramatically.

Population size is often cited as a cause of poverty. And it is true that a large population burdens the limited resources. Yet the problem lies deeper than that. Not every one has equal access or rights to the national resources. Distribution of wealth and resources by the state, in most countries, remains, to put it bluntly, unjust. The inequality in the returns that the poor get for their labour or their products means that they will never be able to break out of this cycle of poverty unless drastic changes take place in the work and remuneration equation. Non-existent fall back mechanisms and "safety nets" for the poor increase their vulnerability to both intra familial and external pressures and events.

With the current economic system and level of corruption that exists in countries such as Bangladesh, even if the population were to halve tomorrow there would still be some very rich and many very poor, for human greed would continue to compel some to appropriate more for themselves and their heirs by fair means or foul.

These are some of the tangible factors that even the children, as young as they are, in our study are able to grasp and connect to their own poor conditions. The other reasons for poverty which some children have referred to are "the rich exploiting the poor," "the rich owning assets to generate further wealth" and "the government not playing its role as it ought to." We believe that before long the children will comprehend the intangibles which indirectly add to, or even cause, the poor conditions they have to live in.

Other Factors Causing and/or Perpetuating Poverty

Poverty within individual families and generations of the family is relatively easier to trace, and much analysis of poverty focuses upon how individual families became poor. It would seem the only commonality between the poor is their present predicament. But poverty is not just about an individual family's misfortune and failings. There are factors that play below the surface that are more difficult to discern, and therefore more difficult to appreciate and address. These causes are beyond individual control, operating at systems and institutional levels. They are often imperceptible, and identifying and tackling these require considerable commitment if poverty is to be eradicated. Both national and international policies and agencies interact and define how resources are generated, made available and accessed. Their ideological bases, or a shift in any of them, have far-reaching consequences, often over a period of time. An analysis of these is essential to understanding the multi-dimensionality of the causes of poverty. The possible solutions for tackling poverty also lie therein.

National policies and strategies: Poverty is not necessarily due to lack of capability, or about hard work. Children's stories tell us about the work and management of meagre resources that they and their parents have to undertake to survive. Yet, despite all their efforts, they and the masses in Bangladesh remain poor. Although Bangladesh itself is a poor country, there is concentration of substantial wealth (and power) in the hands of the few. How does this come about and why is this tolerated in the face of so many living in dire poverty? Many factors, including the economic model in operation in Bangladesh, contribute to the severe disparities existing in the country.

To boost its economic growth, 1980s onward Bangladesh adopted and implemented economic measures that were more open and liberal. Deregulation, structural adjustment, liberalisation of foreign exchange regulations, and lessening of state control in various economic sectors led to the construction of an environment where foreign investment in the country and private enterprise and export market could flourish unfettered. By the 1990s this non-intervention policy started to show results and the economy grew by five per cent. The country's imports also increased substantially.

The impact on poverty reduction, however, from these major changes was marginal. In fact, during this period the rural population became poorer. Urban poverty decreased somewhat with the launch of industries such as the readymade garments and leather products. At the same time, while the wealth of the nation grew, the inequity between the rich and the poor, and the rural and the urban, also increased manifold. Ironically during the 90s—at the height of trade liberalisation— unemployment rose, both in rural and urban areas, while at the same time the actual wages also came down. Yet in the same period the rich got richer. The earnings of the poorest 20 per cent, by 2001, increased by 24 per cent while the richest 20 per cent gained by 60 per cent.[19]

Presently 54 per cent of the rural population lives below the poverty line, causing them to migrate to cities, which, due to lack of skills and illiteracy amongst the migrants, offers them little except survival. The agricultural labourers are the most vulnerable group, 78 per cent of whom live in poverty—landless and jobless, with environmental havoc and degradation on top. All these further add to child poverty, making children more vulnerable to exploitation by various elements in society.

---

[19] Mujeri and Khondker, 2002.

> National policies continue to emphasise foreign investment and the amassing of capital—be it broader roads and highways for more vehicles, urban high-rises, bridges, factories, sports utility vehicles, telecommunications equipment and defence—related products.... Democratise the formulation of our development policies so that these are not informed solely by the elites who are obsessed with catching up with the west and with [private] property, but instead are formed by all citizens who see themselves as stakeholders in a nation that they are proud of.
>
> — Dr. Farida C. Khan, 2003

The situation is even more intensified by the misguided public policies that determine public expenditure on social sector development. Health and education, the two key elements that could help people out of poverty and help build a better future for millions of children, receive far less resources than actually required in Bangladesh. In 1996 the country spent 2.9 per cent of its GNP on education. The average for the low income countries during this year was 3.9 per cent.[20] During 1998-2000, this was reduced to 2.5 per cent of the GDP, most of which was spent upon salaries and administration costs. While the world average expenditure on health is 2.5 per cent, the Bangladesh health sector received only 1.4 per cent of the total GDP during the same period.[21]

There appears to be a lack of serious commitment on the part of successive governments to tackle problems such as corruption at their source, all of which continue to keep the majority of Bangladeshis in impoverished conditions. Corruption amongst providers and institutions, for example, further deprives people of their rights, and prevents the needy from accessing services. Corruption, a serious hindrance to the well-being of the population, but more so for the very poor who cannot really themselves gain from it, remains rampant in all spheres of life. The state appears not only unable to check it but also seems to be implicated in it.

More than often national policies and priorities in Bangladesh, and in other countries in debt to western powers and dependent on aid, are directed by a global agenda that is determined by a few powerful nations. While in the final analysis, a nation's leaders and administrators must take full responsibilities for its successes and failures, it would be fair to suggest that, in the globalised world we live in, few states can claim to have full control over their economic and social development.

---

[20] World Bank, 2000.

[21] http://hdr.undp.org/reports/global/2003/pdf/hdr03_HDI.pdf.

Globalisation and the rich-poor equation: "Globalisation" has become the buzz word of our times and is generally meant to conjure up an image of a world more interconnected and moving towards a freer, more equitable mode of economic, social and political relationships and exchanges between nations and people. It is supposed to signify a world where time and space barriers have been removed, allowing people to enjoy similar or same lifestyles across the globe. Globalisation has been promoted as a sound medium for the poor nations and people in order to become prosperous.

Some of this, to a certain extent, is quite true. Through the internet the latest information on a myriad subjects from around the world is a click away. E-mail and mobile phone technologies have provided connectivity with anyone, most anywhere in the world. In rural Bangladesh, for instance, where there are no phone lines, Grameen Phone has installed mobile phones and, as Mohammad Yunus, the founder of Grameen Bank, claims, connected the back and beyond to the 21st century. Products can be manufactured in any corner of the globe and can reach a world-wide market at a fast rate for a low price. Globalisation

> 1 billion living in the high-income countries have average incomes that are 75 times more than that of the wretched 1.2 billion who barely manage to survive.
>
> — *Wolf, 2003*
>
> In countries of the North the gap between the rich and the poor has also increased manifold.

has provided encompassing technologies through which one can keep tabs from one's own home on what is happening half way across the world; transportation that is fast and cheap thereby increasing phenomenally the number of people jetting around the world; media that covers event that are simultaneously watched around the globe; financial markets that work round the clock.

The concept that all those who share in the globalisation process will reap the benefits, however, remains a pure illusion. Globalisation has clearly failed to improve the lot of the poor anywhere, despite their full participation in the process in a myriad of ways and levels. As farmers, labourers, factory workers, call centre employees and so on, the poor have contributed to accumulation of immense wealth for some but themselves remain hardly any better off. Rather, as all indicators suggest, globalisation has acutely widened the gap between the rich and the poor in the "rich" as well as the "poor" countries. Globalisation has certainly helped poor nations—or rather a small minority, a certain class, within the poor nations—to become rich and ultra rich. The sad fact is that instead of getting a share of the spoils of globalisation, the poor of the world pay a heavy price for the benefits of globalisation, for they have neither influence nor

> The absolute number of those living on $1 per day or less continues to increase. The worldwide total rose from 1.2 billion in 1987 to 1.5 billion today, and if recent trends persist, will reach 1.9 billion by 2015.
>
> — *The World Bank, 2000*

control over what happens, or where and when it happens. They have become, to be more accurate, the victims of its vagaries. It has reduced them to cheap and expendable labour—the modern "coolies"—and their countries to "markets." Moreover, despite all the promises, many countries in the south are lagging well behind the rich world. In truth, with so many odds against them, including starting miles behind in the race, it would be foolhardy to believe that poor countries can ever catch up in this race which has no finishing line.

The thrust for globalisation comes from the countries of the North, looking for new and bigger markets for their ever-expanding production lines and for sources of cheaper raw products and of course cheap labour. Accrued historical and technological advantages enjoyed by the western world and its corporations have been further re-enforced and expanded by "free market" policies—removing national restrictions that hampered growth, expansion and profits of the corporations. Nationally, this included disempowering the trade unions, adjusting taxes and financial requirements, giving licence to the business world to move its operations to any country at any time. Internationally, through the World Bank, the International Monetary Fund (IMF), the World Trade Organisation (WTO) and aid agency programmes, it has involved persuading or even forcing reforms, privatisation and deregulation that pave the path of globalisation. Such measures have had drastic impact on some countries, specifically in Africa, where economies have shrunk or even crumbled.

Globalisation is but another shrewd term for boundaryless, rampant capitalism, with few checks or controls—a modern version of colonisation and imperialism. (After all, the colonisation of countries such as India did start with the East India Company.) Now poor countries are pitted against each other to compete for business investments and aid money from

> 70 per cent of the world trade is now in control of 500 transnational corporations (TNC), mainly western, and some TNCs are now richer than some nation states.

the rich world, and in return they give up their autonomy and power to foreign investors and governments. Examples of national and environmental laws being superseded by multinational corporations abound. Paradoxically, since the 1980s more countries that have come into being have opted for democratic forms of government, yet states and people who voted for the system have less power than ever. The multi-corporation laws rule. What does this spell for democracy?

Multinational companies are becoming transnationals and conglomerates by incorporating businesses round the world within their fold. They can move their operations (or parts of it), with impunity, to countries where labour is cheap, and health and safety as well as environmental legislation weak or non-existent. No sooner is another cheaper source of production discovered than they move on, leaving in their wake unemployment, environmental mess and fractured lives.

> The multinationals are "largely beyond the control of national governments; they can switch production, jobs, capital— and pollution—from country to country to get the regimes that best suit them."
> — *Lean, 2002*

The ideology of free market and de-regulation translates into boundaryless operations for owners and producers. Thus textile workers in Britain are finding life increasingly hard as jobs are being cut and production shifted to other parts of the world. As the managing director of a swimwear/lingerie factory in Nottingham explains, "The workforce has been scaled down from 200 one year ago, with all the high volume business going to cheaper places such as Morocco or China."[22] Currently, Bangladesh's readymade garment industry, which provided jobs in millions for women and boosted their economic status, is also facing a crisis at two levels—one is competition from countries like China that are now within the fold of the free market. The steady move over the last two years of several customers to China has seriously impacted on the industry already. The second is the end of the Multi Fibre Agreement (MFA) in 2004, which allows western governments to impose strict quotas on garment-producing countries. And for Bangladesh, which is heavily reliant on this industry for its foreign exchange, this will be a serious setback. Whatever the loss in terms of the number of jobs, it will be a killing blow to a country already on its knees with poverty, unemployment, debt and aid.

Growth appears to have disproportionately benefited the developing nations, and all indicators suggest that it is the better off people within these nations who have gained the most.

---

[22] *The Daily Star*, 11/9/03.

USA represents 5 per cent of the world's population yet consumes 30 per cent of the world's resources. The standard of living in rich and industrialised countries has risen phenomenally. Second homes, a car for every adult in the family, personal TVs etc. for individuals are now commonplace for most middle class families in the west as well as the wealthy in the poor world.

In 1960 the 20 per cent of the population living in the developed world had 30 times the income of the world's 20 per cent poorest, and today it is 75 times as much.[23]

Globalisation has also depressed the prices of raw commodities and the wages of producers and at the same time increased the profits for the middlemen and the owners.

The shrimp industry in Bangladesh is just one example of the goods that are produced in the poor world cheaply to provide a higher and better standard of living for the rich around the globe at a low cost to them.

Shrimp farming in Bangladesh has been financed by the World Bank, despite evidence of dire environmental and human disaster in countries like India, Vietnam, Thailand, where shrimp farming was taken on a large scale, also funded by the World Bank. The mangrove swamps, where shrimp farming has to be done, is not only important for the nation's ecosystem but also for the world. Yet it is being exploited and destroyed ruthlessly at a rapid rate so people in rich countries can eat more and cheaper shrimps.

The economic gains for the shrimp farmers, meagre as they are, are very short term, for the farms can be operated for a maximum of five years. The pesticides and antibiotics used for farming the shrimp accumulate over years at the bottom of the pond, rendering it unusable after a certain period. Many children work on these farms, standing in the pond water for hours at a time to collect the shrimp. And the losses far outweigh the gains. Once the farms have out-lived their use they have to be abandoned, leaving behind toxic waste which continues to seep into the underground water, leaving communities without any drinking water. Even to wash in this water is hazardous as it causes rashes and other skin problems. Communities are left with little choice but to move—and where else but the city.

Retailers are constantly looking for novel products to satisfy the ever-growing urge of consumers for newer items, and at the same time promoting consumerism as "lifestyle" thereby generating greater trade

---

[23] Kingsnorth, 2003.

and profits. Unfortunately, the labourers, at the bottom of the chain of production and distribution, remain abjectly poor, subsidising the "designer lifestyle" of the rich.

Within the last 15 years, from small livelihood endeavours of the fishing communities, shrimp farming has turned into a $9 billion turnover per annum industry worldwide. The price of shrimp has fallen by 65 per cent during this period, and its consumption in the rich countries has increased 300 per cent. As in all other instances of such transactions, the growers reap the least out of this. The rural communities

> Poor countries rely on commodities for income. Most very rich people do not have incomes; they live off assets. They have benefited enormously from, among other things, lower coffee, copper and cocoa prices, from lower labour costs and from rising asset prices.
>
> — Ann Pettifor, 2003

whose land and environment is polluted for generations to come, and who are now exposed to more severe environmental disasters, who are already, or may soon become, displaced people, continue to live on meagre earnings. Bigger dividends accrue to the middlemen in the urban areas of Bangladesh but the lion's share goes to the wholesalers and supermarkets in the rich countries.

Globally poor countries such as Bangladesh are becoming more dependent on cash crops and manufactured goods for their economic growth, trading of which (including price setting, where it will be purchased from, which country will manufacture them) is controlled by a few corporations in the North, leaving most of these countries and its peoples' fate in the hands of global powers. And since the balance of power already resides with corporations, the World Bank, the IMF and the donors, they are able to dictate the terms and conditions of trade and aid,

> 70% of the world trade is now in control of 500 transnational corporations (TNC), mainly western, and some TNC are richer than some nation states.

further weakening the poor countries. While this situation, in most cases, works in favour of the elites in the countries of the South, its impacts on the vast majority—and particularly the population already living in poverty—is devastating, making them poorer and destitute. A major proportion of population in many of these countries is below the age of 15.

> On the streets of Dhaka a blind man and his wife play string instruments and sing traditional songs and make around 50-60 taka a day which feeds their family of 6.

(In Bangladesh children between the ages of 0 to 15 constitute 40 per cent of the population.) Wars, internal strife and discrimination, occupation of states by the more powerful, further add to the plight of the poverty-stricken people, including vast numbers of children.

> The Iraq invasion has cost the USA government $50 billion to date (summer 2003) and will incur an expenditure of approximately $3 billion spending per month for the duration of the occupation.

Levels of Poverty and Deprivation in a World of Plenty: Some Alarming Facts

- 600 million children, worldwide, exist on under $1 per day;
- In rich countries 47 million children live in poverty: USA (22.4%), Britain (19.8%), and Canada (15.5%);
- Around 250 million children between the ages of 5 to 14 are economically active —doing jobs that often cripple their bodies, stunt their growth and shorten their lives;
- As many as 39% (209 million) of the children under the age of 5 in developing countries are stunted—Bangladesh: 55%;
- Nearly 2 million children die every year from diarrhoeal and other water-related diseases;
- There are 31 million children who are displaced worldwide as refugees;
- Over the last 20 years the number of people living in poverty has increased to more than 1.2 billion (20% of the world population lives in absolute poverty).

Contrast Between the Rich and the Poor

- One-third of the world's population cannot afford essential drugs. In poor countries of Africa and Asia it is 50%;
- The top eight pharmaceuticals in the world (USA) spend in the region of 50,000 million dollars on advertising and promotion of their products;
- For the poorest 10% in Bangladesh the national income share is 4.1%. For the richest 10% the share is 23.7%;
- For the poorest 10% in USA the income share is 1.5%; for the richest 10% the share is 28.5%;
- The three richest people in the world have wealth that surpasses the joint gross domestic product of the 48 poorest countries;

- The richest countries, representing 15% of the world population, consume 56% of the world's resources while 11% is consumed by 40% of the people living in poorest countries;
- The average African now consumes 20% less than 25 years ago.

Other
- More than 1 billion people lack access to clean water;
- 2.5 billion people lack sanitation facilities;
- 800 million people in the world remain illiterate.

Development aid, government and non-government organisations: Like globalisation, "aid" thrives on the myth that it helps the poor. And Bangladesh is a classic example of how little aid has helped uplift the country from poverty. After more than 30 years of intervention from donors and various national and international non-government organisations (NGOs), Bangladesh remains one of the poorest countries in the world with a myriad of problems gnawing its people. We would like to suggest that aid, loans tied to various conditions, and the voluntary sector working with no over all co-ordination, are in themselves one of the problems for countries like Bangladesh.

> Fifty years of development experience have yielded four critical lessons. First, macroeconomic stability is an essential prerequisite for achieving the growth needed for development. Second, growth does not trickle down; development must address human needs directly. Third, no one policy will trigger development; a comprehensive approach is needed. Fourth, institutions matter; sustained development should be rooted in processes that are socially inclusive and responsive to changing circumstances.
>
> — *World Bank, 2000*

The donor programmes are very much dependent on the geopolitical agenda of the donor countries, and aid it seems has become a tool to facilitate globalisation. On the back of each aid programme come many businesses and enterprises. Along with some social, technical and welfare reforms, aid donors and financial institutions, by and large, try to bring about systems, structural and process changes similar to those that exist in the rich world to create universal conditions in which corporate interests can flourish. The World Bank and IMF loans to the country always demand structural or other changes that may not necessarily be in line with what the national policymakers may deem useful. But the piper calls the tune.

Speaking of the influence exerted by the World Bank, IMF and other aid-givers on internal policies, Novak argues that "no government could long stand against the combined dislike of all the national and international aid-givers. Not only do these viceroys of charity dictate the country's microeconomic policy .... They dictate where and when bridges are built, such as the recent debate over the Jamuna Bridge and they determine the duties to be charged on import."[24] Many Bangladeshi businesses as well as academics are also highly critical of the donors for their excessive interference in policy matters. It is argued that the taxpayers contribute three times as much as the donors, yet wield hardly any influence on decision-making. It is also felt that although the amount of donor assistance has decreased over the years, their intrusion into policy matters has in fact increased. The World Bank, as the co-ordinator of the donors, is seen as "too interfering."

Bangladesh is inundated with NGOs—big and small, encompassing rural and urban divisions and sub-divisions. Their work covers every conceivable area. They are involved from agriculture to education, health and family planning to zoo maintenance. While certain gains have been made, over all, given the amount of time, energy, expertise and money that goes in, the results are disappointing. While all types of issues are being tackled in a variety of manners, the fundamental problem of poverty—which is the root cause of so many other areas of concern—continues unabated.

Ali's father died when he was about six, leaving him and his mother at the mercy of relatives. His uncle, who could have afforded to provide some support, did not want to know. Ali's mother took on sewing work but could not earn enough to feed the two of them. At the age of 7 Ali ended up in Dhaka, selling balloons for survival. Now thirteen, he still lives on the streets, vulnerable to exploitation and harassment. Ali's situation raises serious questions with regard to the effectiveness and efficiency of the numerous NGOs and government agencies working in the rural areas. In the last 30 years a major effort has gone into developing the rural economy and supporting the population in various ways in Bangladesh. With a heavy concentration of donor programmes, and the Government and NGOs to carry out such operations, it is surprising that as yet there is no safety net for people such as Ali and his mother.

---

24 Novak, 1994.

As many of the NGOs are run on funds from foreign agencies (some receiving as much as 50 to 100 per cent of their funding) they also have to adopt certain systems and processes and abide by certain schemes. This often means that despite their local knowledge, most NGO work is more project focused and service related, ignoring issues of human rights or a holistic approach. Also rather than a co-ordinated approach there is competition and overlap amongst these agencies. In some places the population is suffering from aid fatigue while other areas remain without support. All the same, positive changes have come about through their work but there are two grave concerns: some NGOs have become unwieldy and bureaucratic, somewhat removed from their constituency—much like the government; more money is spent on the administration than on the beneficiaries. They are also becoming more commercial, thereby losing the spirit of community organisation, participation and inclusion. The issues of accountability and transparency are also becoming casualties. The other problem is corruption within the organisations. Only a small proportion of money allocated to the projects is actually spent on them.

Over the years the government in Bangladesh has become severely aid dependent. Yet not all aid goes to the poor, or those in most need. For a start, 75% of the aid returns to the donor countries by way of consultant fees, equipment (purchased mainly from the donor country) and administration. Of the remaining 25 per cent, it is estimated that 75% never reaches those for whom it was intended.

> In the last 32 years, hundreds of thousands of crores of taka have been brought from abroad to this country by the government and non-government organisations as loans and grants. Regrettably much of these huge sums of money were looted by a few thousand individuals and they have become unbelievably rich over a very short span of time.
>
> — The Daily Star 21/9/03

The gap between the rich and poor—just as in the better off countries—is increasing and all indications are that it will continue to do so, particularly in Bangladesh. At a material level the scale and magnitude of poverty in rich countries may be very different from places like Bangladesh. But without an extensive comparative study it is difficult to assess the socio-psychological impact of poverty and all it entails for impoverished people of rich and poor nations. But one thing is perhaps certain that with the social welfare system established in developed

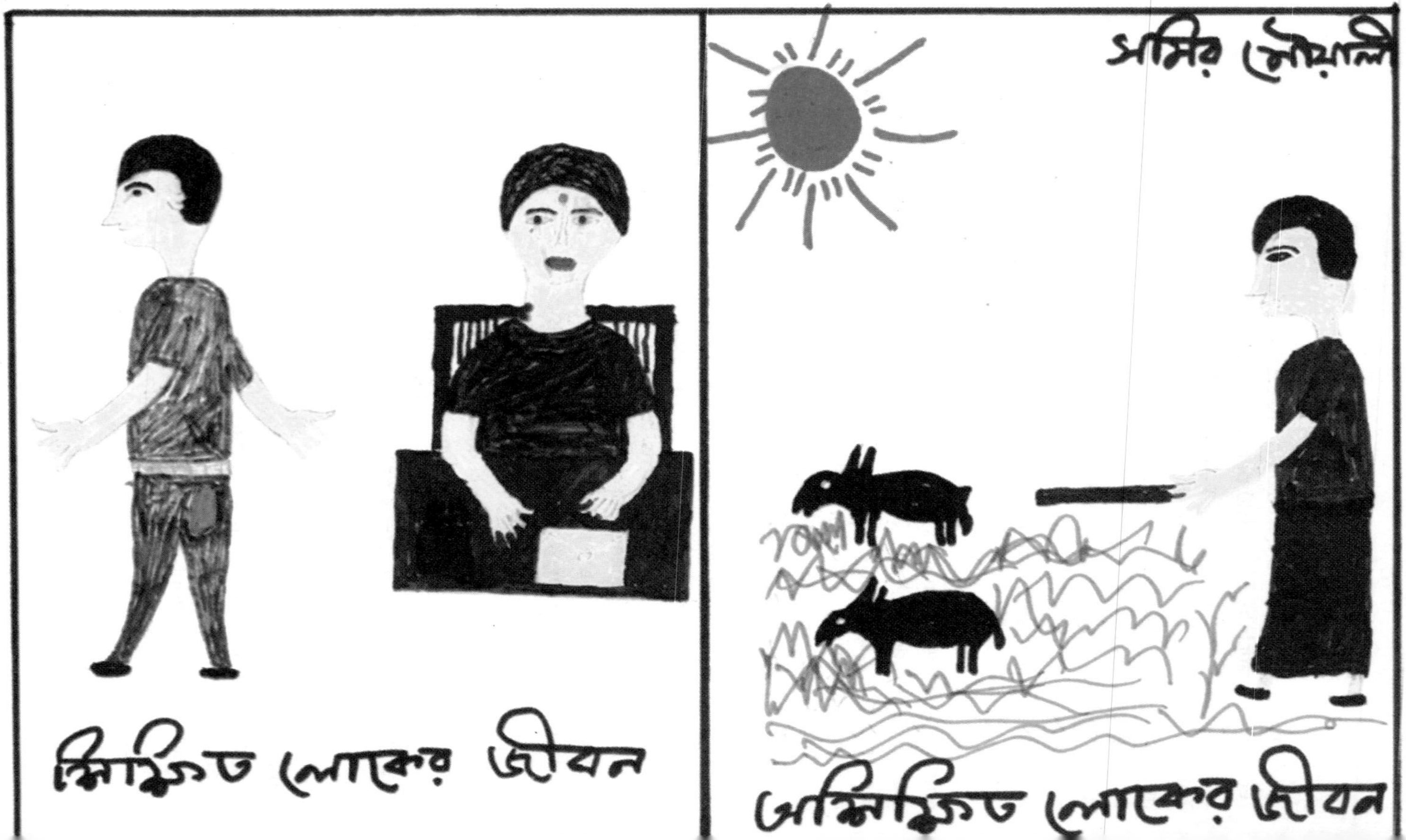
সমির ভৌয়ালী
শিক্ষিত লোকের জীবন
অশিক্ষিত লোকের জীবন

countries at least the poor know they will get some assistance if needed. In Bangladesh the poor have to rely on the charity of the rich, and on family, friends and neighbours.

However, the primary responsibility of ensuring that funding is not misused or misappropriated by its own or the NGOs or the donor personnel lies with the government of the country. In the same way the onus is on the government for good governance and equity for all its citizens, for the betterment of the many living on the margins of the society, for the creation of a civic culture where the poor and their children are assisted out of poverty and not exploited and abused. But too many people at all levels are busy with other priorities (often those which bring personal gains) to worry too much about thousands of street children, most of whom struggle on without any support, or about seven million children working from a very young age, or high numbers of children dropping out of primary schools as their parents cannot afford to buy uniforms and books, or thousands upon thousands of girls and boys surviving on one meal a day (and often none) with far-reaching implications for their health, development and learning.

CHAPTER 6

CONCLUSIONS AND IMPLICATIONS

Consequences of childhood poverty are harsh and have a long-term impact on the individual and the society at large. In their most formative years—physical, emotional, cognitive and social—for a colossal number of children across the world there is no childhood, only malnutrition, lack of living and play space, deficit of education, and lack of respect and care from people with means in society. The result is poor health, low or no educational achievement, work from a very early age, often separation from parents, and life on the margins.

Child poverty is an emotive subject, the topic of many debates and the focus of many development programmes. To understand the plight of children living in poverty, one has to gain insight into the lives of their families and communities that endure deprivation and destitution, in most cases, over generations. Equally important is to recognise that the general notions held about people living in poverty often inform the policies to tackle poverty or become an excuse to discount the issue all together.

Myths and Realities Around the Poor

"We must stop unduly wasting scarce resources on the lazy, illiterate masses and instead try to help the industrialists, entrepreneurs and businessmen—the people who have proved that they are competent and capable of improving their own fortunes and thereby those of the nation itself" This comment by a professor of a prestigious university in Dhaka shows how our beliefs shape our image of the poor and of poverty. These beliefs are mostly acquired through the generalisation of individual experiences, either our own or those of others. Or, they are developed to protect our own selves and our sensibilities. Prevailing political and economic ideologies also play a major part in shaping our views. No matter how they are developed, our reactions to the poor are based on how we perceive them.

The conversations with the children in this book, however, provide contrasts to some of these commonly held beliefs.

All poor are the same: The poor are the same but only in the predicament that they all find themselves in. Poverty is their reality. But how they came to be poor, what their experiences are, and how they react to them are all different. As individuals their lives are shaped by their personal experiences, the skills that they have, their abilities to gather and utilise resources and so are their desires, aspirations and vision.

The poor are poor due to their own fault: The children in these stories were not born in rich families, neither were their parents. There was no wealth to be squandered away in the first place. Ill health, lack of jobs, death, depletion or loss of resources pushed people further and further into deprivation. A person's life chances are determined by where in the world and in the family he or she is born. These were already poor or extremely vulnerable families, where one incident caused the family to slip into the quicksand of poverty. "From rags to riches" stories abound. But in reality, for the majority, if you are born in a poor country into a poor family, 99 per cent chances are that you will remain poor or get poorer, deprived of many basic rights enshrined in various constitutions and charters.

The poor are lazy: It is clearly evident from the children's stories that they and their families work extremely hard for survival and are willing to take chances to improve their conditions. All the parents, and some of the children, are engaged in back-breaking physical work, as rickshaw pullers or domestic servant. Many of the families gave up the security of their community and moved from their village to the city to make a living. But no matter how hard they toil, better living eludes them for the remunerations, for their labour, are so very low.

The poor do not desire education: Except for one child, all the children in these stories come from families where the parents themselves are not educated but want their children to acquire education. Both parents and children work hard so that the children can continue in school. When survival becomes even more of a struggle, or when the expected returns from education seem to diminish in comparison to gains from entry into the work force, schooling will be discontinued. If parents cannot find the work to feed and educate their children, if the educational system is not flexible enough for working children, then there is no choice but to opt out of the formal learning process.

Children from poor families lack knowledge and awareness: The children in these stories demonstrate their awareness of the world, its inequalities and how these are perpetuated. They can analyse the causes of poverty and disparities. Their knowledge of the lives of the rich shows that the rich might not be aware of how the poor people live, but their own lives and lifestyles are clearly visible to those on the other side of the fence.

The poor want to be rich and at any cost: The children in these stories are aware of how wealth is acquired, both by fair and unfair means. They know education and hard work are essential for progress in life. With the exception of a couple, all that the majority of the children want are a comfortable life with fewer worries; a clean home and surrounding environment; and the ability to provide food and education for their families. To achieve these they are prepared to work hard.

The poor only want money: The poor need money—to buy food, for shelter and clothes. But the children in their conversations reveal that more than money they want respect. They feel that they might not have money, but they have the intelligence and the capability. They are poor not because of their own fault, but because of the way the world operates. Where inequality is rampant and deprivation a given, sensitivity and appreciation on the part of those who seem to have it all would make it possible to live life with some dignity.

> Sarmin's story and other such narrations in the book tell us that the poor are neither lazy nor do they lack skills or resourcefulness. They are ready to work hard to improve their own conditions and are prepared to sacrifice much to educate their children so that they can have a better future. However, when caught in the poverty trap, people have few choices. In fact the choice is between survive or perish, between starvation and bits of scraps, between rudimentary shelter and sleeping on the streets. The poor do not control their country's economy or politics, nor do they have any influence over the world systems and developments e.g. globalisation. So it is not out of choice that they make their children work at home, or outside, from a tender age. It is not lack of love and care either; it is simply a way of managing abject poverty.

Reducing Poverty: Who does it?

There is no doubt that national and international institutions have put in considerable thought and resources into tackling poverty. However, as mentioned earlier, poverty, if anything, is on the increase—even in the rich world. What is urgently needed is a programme of action that deals with the fundamental causes of poverty and not simply with its consequences and manifestations—a programme with the victims of poverty playing a key role in its development.

The testimony from the children tells us that the poor are more than willing to work hard and to take risks to better their own and their families' lives.

Uncertainties that abound in the day-to-day life of the poor and affect their existence in complex ways are rarely evident to those who have not experienced poverty. Besides the physical consequences of inadequate food intake and ill health, poverty converts the psychological make-up of the people. The risks and uncertainties that plague their lives change the way they perceive themselves and their position in the world. The continued marginalisation and second-class treatment that the poor get by the rich and the powerful erodes the feeling of self worth. Children sense this lack of respect and often start to internalise this from

> Frederick Temple, World Bank Country Director for Bangladesh, "Poverty is multi-dimensional, going well beyond monetary income to include education, health and nutrition; risk and vulnerability; crime and violence; and powerlessness and absence of voice. Reducing poverty therefore is about social transformation, and needs a comprehensive framework."
>
> — UNCRC, Article 27

an early age. Poverty forces people, both children and their parents, to take on any kind of work available. This entry into any obtainable activity, from pulling rickshaws and vans, to scouring the rubbish dumps, does not allow for either the use of existing skills or development of potentially more beneficial ones. The poor continue to live on the margins of the society, represented, if at all, only by their votes in the general or civic body election. Neither their interests nor their voices are heard in any of the decision-making bodies.

Yet, like the rest of us, they think and analyse, have ideas and visions and speculate about their own and their children's future. And the children contributing to this book have placed a high premium on education as a tool to tackling poverty. They and their parents are willing to make sacrifices so that education can be attained. What they are therefore looking for is easily accessible: a flexible and free education system with no hidden costs attached to it.

But it needs to be emphasised that neither the children nor their parents are looking for charity or handouts. They are doing and are willing to do whatever is required to better their situation for they strongly believe that self help is the best help. All the same, they know that the levels of poverty they and so many others live in requires— beyond their hard work and the strategy of spending wisely, keeping away from bad habits and saving—serious action from the government and from the rich (both at home and abroad). They argue that the government must initiate more projects to enable the poor to stand on their own feet, create more jobs, provide land and ensure that the aid that comes from abroad gets distributed properly.

Population reduction is seen as another key factor to reducing poverty and the children are themselves planning to have no more than two children each.

It is clear that what the children are asking of the government and the rich is initiatives and actions that will help them continue with their aspiration of self-help and their commitment to work. This, they believe, will help them out of the economic predicament and destitution that they find themselves in.

The children have also highlighted the upheaval caused by migration from village to city as well as pointed out some of the reasons for the move. Many of them would prefer to live in their villages, within their communities. Rural development, which would boost the rural economy and infrastructure as well as provide a livelihood and long-term safety and security, would help tempt the children and their families back to their roots. Corruption, another reality blighting the lives and future of the poor, was raised by the children. This is an area which not only requires radical thinking but also absolute commitment on the part of the government to tackle this problem within its own ranks and at all levels of the system.

The point that needs to be raised is when will the government and society listen to these children's voices, tap into this verve and willingness, find ways of supporting their initiative and self-reliance and reward them appropriately for their contribution to the economy and development of the country?

The constitutions of each country provide the framework within which specific policies are formulated and implemented. Some of these charters or conventions are aimed at reducing inequalities by removing barriers to access and use of resources. Once again the question that arises is why, with decades of policies and efforts on part of national and local government and NGOs, poverty keeps increasing and the gap between the rich and poor keeps growing?

It is about time that the government of Bangladesh and other poor countries conduct an in-depth comprehensive analysis of national systems and international programmes to understand how these contribute to inequalities and what would be the best way to re-structure these. The fact that policy makers rarely ask or include the people experiencing poverty to contribute to the solutions to their plight needs to be addressed for anti-poverty programmes to have a real and lasting impact. Children living in poverty, in particular, are even more marginalised, as some children from the slums point out:

> We, the slum children, cannot enter the programmes in the city where beautifully adorned children from the privileged class sing and dance. They talk about child rights in those programmes as the government does. But we do not understand heavy words like "Child Rights," "Education for All" or "Food for Education." What we realise is that we lack food, housing, school facilities and play grounds.[25]

Governments also need to take measures to help equitable distribution of resources and wealth. For example, creation of specific wealth taxes, or poverty taxes or higher taxes on second and third cars or homes could generate income which could be ploughed back into anti-poverty programmes and help build a basic welfare system for the most vulnerable and in need. The state and the rich have to recognise that internal stability is dependent upon equitability that exists within the country. A divided society, with high levels of disparity of wealth and rights, does not bode well for the future of a nation or beyond.

NGOs and other development organisations need to think why it is that the money that gets poured into programmes to alleviate child and adult poverty is unable to yield results. Is it, because of the enormity of the problem or, because it is not being targeted properly? Or because the problem of child poverty has deeper roots in adult poverty, and adult poverty will persist unless people are given opportunities and fair returns for their labour and produce? It needs to be examined why, while there are such few employment opportunities for adults, the numbers of working children seem to multiply. The children in their stories have very vividly detailed the physical and psychological hardships of their working lives. The children require safeguard from labour that damages them for life.

We know from the children and their parents that, as far as the families are concerned, sending children to work is not their first choice.

---

[25] Murshed, 2003.

When caught in a poverty trap, people have few choices. The choice then is between "survive" or "perish." While the challenge is to persuade children away from work and put them in school, it would be prudent to provide some alternatives for survival first, like living wages for adults, wages on which they can actually sustain their families. Simply banning child labour will not help matters either. The garments industry's abolition of child labour in Bangladesh and its consequences provide some lessons on dealing with child labour. International rules and regulations have to be understood in the local context and implemented with local partners. A system to support the children and their families has to be in place before the abolition is enforced. In the absence of carefully thought-through consequences and actions, children can end up on the streets in far worse conditions than they were in before. Externally imposed sanctions rarely solve the problems. They set up a rigid and artificial set of rules which only serve to hide the problems. Companies find ways around them, and, once this subversion takes place, it becomes twice as difficult to address the issues.

Individual families make their own efforts and create ways to subsist on whatever is possible. Life for these children is a hard struggle, but they try to deal with adversity and make the most under the given circumstances. Even the ones with initiative and drive, as people in our study, who uprooted themselves and families, moved from rural to urban areas, find that improvement in life is marginal. Instead of no job they manage to pick up some work whatsoever—going through the rubbish heap is also a job. Instead of starving they get one to two meals a day. But their potential remains unrealised for their starting point is zero or minus zero—no education, no inherited wealth or status or any other advantages. An effort has to be made to make these children stakeholders in their country and its future. Else generations will be lost and with them, their creativity, skills and potential.

While the children consider education as one of the main routes out of poverty, the current educational process mostly serves as a divisive rather than a cohesive force. We as observers, mediators, facilitators, can never get to the depth of the desperation of the poor or fully appreciate their needs and desires and their sense of separation from the world that has much maligned, marginalised and exploited them. It is not just goods and opportunities that are beyond their reach, it is also people who reside in the world of wealth and plenty. Any meaningful contact or relationship between the two worlds of the rich and poor in the current context is simply out of question. Yet education could be made a bridge if the rich and their offspring were sensitised to the causes of poverty, its manifestations and effects. Education could also promote the development of a social conscience, whereby one's role in unequal and unnecessary consumption of resources and one's contribution to both causes and solutions to reduce poverty could be examined. Thus simply educating the poor will not resolve the issue of poverty. Education for all about poverty is required. Reduction and eradication of poverty cannot be just about educating the poor. It requires education for the rest also. Simply educating the poor, or looking for economic solutions will not solve the problem. Many things have to go hand in hand including social development and fair prices and wages for producers and workers.

Without fundamental transformation in our thinking regarding rich-poor relations, those both between richer and poorer nations and between poor and affluent people, not much will change for the people living in poverty. For, as outlined in the previous chapter, global "free market" policies and programmes, aid providers' hidden self-serving schemes and the government and NGOs' reformist agendas

> **Dropping the Debt!**
>
> In 2000, the debt of billions of dollars, owed by the poor countries to the rich world, was annulled. However, as the record for the last four years shows, cancellation of debts changed little in poor countries due to a number of conditions attached to this act.
>
> Debts have mounted again, leaving the poor world where it was, beholden to the rich.

impact both indirectly and directly on the lives of the poor, often intensifying rather than reducing poverty.

A reduction in poverty will require radical steps on the part of, amongst others, national and multinational corporations, for example, the strategy of sharing profits with workers. The WTO and the IMF will also have to examine the impact of the conditions they impose on poor countries. WOT and IMF rules clearly run against the interest of the South countries. These countries will have to unite and challenge the unjust rules that favour the rich world, and fight for other common benefits such fair prices for raw and manufactured products. National governments could also take other bold measures like setting a minimum wage for the work force.

As Kulsum and Jahanara, two of the girls working the rubbish dumps, pointedly suggest, neither the journalists, who wrote an article on their plight, nor the NGO workers, society in general or the government have done much to bring about any change in these children's or the impoverished adults' lives. Poverty together with globalisation is a large-scale, worldwide phenomenon. Economic growth or "development" alone cannot address the causes or problems of poverty. What is needed is social restructuring and a more equitable remuneration and distribution of resources.

Last Words

The poor are not people on whose behalf we have to eat $500-a-plate dinners; they need the dinners. They are not people for whom we the better off "need to do good;" they need to be involved in their own betterment. The poor are not there for others to make careers and money out of their lives. They do not need new buzz words to describe or sanitise their condition and situation but want actions that involve them from the outset, action that starts with and based on their views and needs (as defined by them) and not imposed by governments, NGOs or rich donors interested in furthering their own agendas behind the mask of development, change and poverty alleviation.

The children in these stories are prepared for a long struggle to create a comfortable life for themselves and their families. They also seem quite committed to a life of honesty to get what they desire. One can sense the frustration in some children against the unjust ways of the world. This anger does not seem to be directed at the rich in particular but at the circumstances they find themselves in. In a world where injustice and exploitation are so prevalent and visible to the children from such an early age, and unfair means so rewarding, it is uncertain to what extent they will be able to adhere to the path of sincerity and honesty.

Bangladesh, along with other countries, has signed the UN Convention on the Rights of the Child in 1990, promising all its children:

- Freedom from violence, abuse, hazardous employment, exploitation, abduction or sale;
- Freedom from hunger and protection from diseases;
- Free compulsory primary education;
- Adequate health care;
- Equal treatment regardless of gender, race or cultural background;

- The right to express opinions and freedom of thought in matters affecting them;
- Safe exposure/access to leisure, play, culture and art.

Unless there is a fundamental response to poverty from the world institutions, states and society, the above outlined rights, and the very basic human right to adequate food and shelter, will remain a dream for most of the children and their future generations. Poverty is not created by the poor. It is a product of the system. And this state of affairs, with two-thirds of the world living in dire conditions, is not just due to the incompetent system of one nation, or only because of the corrupt ways and acquisitiveness of one people one country. The greed and dishonest practices of the privileged and powerful, from the rich and the poor world, are major contributors to global poverty. It is vital to build a momentum across a spectrum of power and opinion towards changing the rules of global trade, demanding fair price for products and fair wages for workers across the globe.

As Mahatma Gandhi said, "There is enough in the world for everyone's need but not enough for one person's greed."

Fleas dream of buying themselves a dog;
and nobodies dream of escaping poverty:
that one magical day good luck will suddenly rain down
on them
- will rain down in buckets.
But good luck doesn't rain down yesterday, today,
tomorrow, or ever.
Good luck doesn't even fall in a fine drizzle,
no matter how hard the nobodies summon it.

— *Eduardo Galeano*

BIBLIOGRAPHY

Alam, Shahidul (2001) *When Dollars Swim Freely*, New Internationalist, 332, March 2001.

Bangladesh Bureau of Statistics (1999) *Census of Slum Areas and Floating Population: 1997, Vol. 1.*

____ (1998) *Urban Poverty Monitoring Survey*: April 1997.

____ (1997) *Summary Report of the Household Expenditure Survey*: 1995-96.

____ (1996) *Report on National Sample Survey of Child Labour in Bangladesh*: 1995-96.

Bangladesh Rural Advancement Committee (BRAC) (1986) *The Net: Power Structure in Ten Villages*, (Rural Study Series 02), Dhaka, BRAC Prokashana, 2nd edition.

Blanchet, Thérèse (1996) *Lost Innocence Stolen Childhoods*. The University Press Limited, Dhaka.

Brazier, Chris (2001) *Building up the Poor—or Reinforcing Inequality?* New Internationalist, 332, March 2001.

Centre for Policy Dialogue (2001) *Poverty Reduction and Globalisation*, Report No. 41.

____ (1999) *Population Development and Urbanisation: The Emerging Issues,* Report No. 16.

Ehsan, Khaleda (2001) *Child Rights: Reality and Challenges*, A Study by Shishu Adhikar Sangjog, Ch. 7, Children and Education.

Gaag, Nikki van der (1999) *Poverty: Challenging the Myths*, New Internationalist, 310, March 1999).

Jabeen, Tahera (2002) *GO-NGO Interventions and Services for Street Children in Dhaka City*, Grameen Trust.

Kingsnorth, Paul (2003) *Do We Need Nature? A Modest Answer*, New Statesman, 9/6/2003.

Mahbub ul Haq (2001) *Human Development in South Asia: Globalisation and Human Development*, Human Development Centre, The University Press Limited, Dhaka.

Mujeri M & Khondker B (2002) *Poverty Implications of Trade Liberalization in Bangladesh: A General Equilibrium Approach*

Nath S R (2002) *Education Watch: Literacy in Bangladesh: Need for a New Vision.*

New Internationalist (2003) *Big Pharma Facts*, November 2003, 362.

Novak, James (1994)—*Bangladesh: Reflections on the Water*, The University Press Limited, Dhaka.

Pettifor, Ann (2003) "Coming soon: the new poor," *Newstatesman*, 1/9/03.

Pilger, John (2003) *The New Rulers of the World*, Verso.

Reeves, Richard (2003) *"Brown's stealth socialism has backfired: Public opinion is now more Tory than ever,"* Newstatsman, 15/9/03.

Thomas, Mark (2003) Columns, Newstatesman, 6/10/2003.

Transparency International-Bangladesh Chapter (2002) *Corruption in Bangladesh' Surveys: An Overview.*

Unicef (2000) *The Progress Report of Nations.*

_____ (1999) *Situation Assessment and Analysis of Children and Women in Bangladesh*; December 1999.

_____ (1999) *A Study on Urban Poverty*; UNICEF Bangladesh; Dhaka.

_____ (2003) The State of the World's Children 2003, Bangladesh.

United Nations Development Programme (2003) *Human Development Report*

Weitzman, Michael, MD (2003) *Low Income and Its Impact on Psychosocial Child Development*; Academy of Pediatrics Centre for Child Health Research and University of Rochester School of Medicine and Dentistry, USA; Published online April 2003

Wolfenshon, J D (2000) Memorandum of the President of the International Development Association and the International Finance Corporation, 2000.

World Bank (2000) Entering the 21st Century, World development report 1999/2000.

Papers

Ahmad, Q K (2003) Ruling neo-liberalism, stumbling poverty reduction: I, *The Daily Star*, October 10, 2003.

_____ (2003) Ruling neo-liberalism, stumbling poverty reduction: II, *The Daily Star*, October 17, 2003.

Ahmed L A (2001) Down in the Dumps, *The Daily Star* (Magazine), August 10, 2001.

Akter Faruk Shahin (2003) Encroaching and taking over the land and property of the tribal people in recent times has become a common occurrence highlighted by this report, *The Daily Star*, August 2, 2003.

Dr. Farida C. Khan (2003) Rethinking Development, *The Independent,* July 22, 2003.

Islam, Sohel (2003) Dhaka gets AQI, *The Daily Star,* July 20, 2003.

Lean, Geoffrey (2002) What kills 2.2 million people a year? *Independent on Sunday* August 25, 2002—(UK).

Mahreen A, Ahmed L A (2002) Victims of a heartless society, *The Daily Star* (Magazine) October 25, 2002.

Majumdar, Badiul Alam (2003) What will happen to the Dukhimon Begums? *The Daily Star* 2003.

Murshed S. K. (2003) Education and Health Care, *The Daily Star,* September 1, 2003.

Rahman, Sultana (2003) Foraging for survival in the open *The Daily Star,* October 5, 2003.

_____ (2003) Persistent poverty perpetuates human trafficking, *The Daily Star,* September 1, 2002.

Rejaul Karim Byron (2003) Cars, foreign tours, ACs to fight poverty, *The Daily Star,* August 23, 2003.

Skeem M (2002) Children of the Tanneries, *The Daily Star* (Magazine), October 18, 2002.

Shahin, Akter Faruk (2003) Persecution and poverty force them to flee home, *The Daily Star,* August 2, 2003.

Staff Correspondent (2003) When death looks greener than starvation, *The Daily Star,* July 24, 2003.

Steven, Morris (2003) Pip Squeak for Coxes and Bramleys, Why we eat this way, *The Guardian: Food,* May 17, 2003, Issue 2.

The Daily Star (2003) City Desk, Is Dhaka Deafening? July 20, 2003.

_____ (2003) National Survey on Child Labour, November 25, 2003.

_____ (2003) Textile workers' tales of woe, BBC Online, September 11, 2003.

_____ (2003) 24 of 28 Docs shunted out for absence: DG health surprised at surprise visit to NICVD, October 3, 2003.

_____ (2003) Accommodating Dhaka: Rise in Urban Population, June 25, 2003.

Zaman M, Ahsan S & Hussain A (2002) An Eid in the lives of ordinary people, *The Daily Star* (Magazine), November 29, 2002.

Websites

http://www.indymedia.ie/newswire.php?story_id=66352&time_posted_upper_li mit=1093665600&time_posted_lower_limit=1093579200.

http://www.globalmarch.org/cl-around-the-world/little-maids-of-dhaka1.php3.

http://www.unicef.org/bangladesh/children_355.htm.
http://www.pediatrics.org/cgi/content/full/1081/44.
http://web.worldbank.org/WBSITE/EXTERNAL/NEWS/.
http://www.cwa.tnet.co.th/booklet/Bangladesh.htm.
http://www.freethechildren.org/campaigns/cl_us.html).
http://www.sdnpbd.org/sdi/international_day/childrens_day/ipec.htm.